P9-ASK-319

FORTNUM & MASON

EST 1707

THE COOK BOOK

TOM PARKER BOWLES

Photography by DAVID LOFTUS

4th ESTATE • *London*

4th Estate
An imprint of HarperCollins*Publishers*
1 London Bridge Street
London SE1 9GF
www.4thEstate.co.uk

First published in Great Britain by 4th Estate in 2016

1 3 5 7 9 8 6 4 2

Design by BLOK
www.blokdesign.co.uk

Typeset by GS Typesetting

A catalogue record for this book is available from the British Library

ISBN 978-0-00-819936-4

Printed in Germany by Mohn Media Mohndruck GMBH

‘Where the food is just about as good as food can be’

F
M

Introduction

They say you never forget your first time. And when it comes to Fortnum & Mason, they'd be right. It was a chill winter's evening, in the early days of the 80s, and I was dressed in my London best – shiny Clarks sandals, pressed corduroy trousers and an unusually spotless shirt. My tattered Husky had been replaced with a dark blue overcoat, and as my cousin and I walked down Piccadilly with my grandmother, I shivered with a mixture of cold, and pure, unalloyed excitement. We were up to see the Christmas windows. And maybe – if we were very good and said our pleases and thank yous and didn't moan or fidget or fiddle about – maybe we could have a banana split at the legendary Fountain.

Having grown up in the depths of Wiltshire, I thought of London as a glittering Emerald City, impossibly exotic, endlessly exciting. And the Italian restaurants, Mimmo's and La Fontana, that my grandmother loved so much were pure bliss. We would suck down endless Coca-Colas, fight with breadstick swords, devour vast bowls of spaghetti Bolognese, and have our cheeks pinched until they glowed. We didn't go out to restaurants in the country. In fact, I don't think Chippenham had any, save the ubiquitous chippy.

London was thrilling, no doubt about that. And Fortnum & Mason was the very pinnacle of big-city glamour. Those spectacular windows, warm and lavish, with the ornate tins of tea and exotic sweets and glittering bottles filled with magic potions. And the clock, where, on the hour, two wooden men emerged, one with a tea tray, the other with a candelabra, faced each other, and bowed graciously.

Of course, I had little idea that these four-foot figures were Mr Fortnum and Mr Mason and that the clock, unveiled in 1964, had taken three years to build. For me, it was utterly magical, more Narnia than Piccadilly, with all the fur wraps and fake snow and sugar-dusted Turkish delight that came with it. Although, unlike Narnia, there was no doubt it was Christmas. 'Hark the Herald Angels' trilled from some hidden speaker, and the place was laden with candied fruits, gleaming decorations and vast, extravagant crackers. The White Witch would not have approved.

There was a smell of spice and tea and expensive eaux de toilette. We fought our way through the festive hordes, past the tailcoated staff (more soldiers than shop assistants) and found ourselves in the Fountain, where that banana split, with its lashings of cream and fruit and chocolate and ice cream, seemed impossibly big. It was lust at first sight. As it had been for my mother and father, and for generations of excitable, star-struck children.

Because Fortnum & Mason is so much more than a mere shop. It's a national icon, a British institution, the finest grocer of them all. For this is a store that has fuelled the furnaces of British history, helped build empires, and fed the appetites of kings and queens, maharajahs and tsars, emperors, dukes and divas alike.

To read through a list of Fortnum's clients is to wander through our island story, a definitive Who's Who of the grand, gilded and great. Every British monarch since Anne, the last reigning Stuart queen. Prime ministers from Gladstone and Disraeli onwards. The most brilliant of war leaders, Wellington, Churchill and Montgomery. Actors from Sir John Gielgud to Sir Michael Caine. Plus some of the greatest writers ever to put pen to paper: Byron, Dickens, James, Conrad, Wodehouse, Betjeman and Waugh. All came for their hampers, griottes, Scotch eggs, smoked salmon, claret and tea. All united in their love for this legendary store.

Fortnum's is a company built upon spent wax. Literally. A seemingly malleable base for such an august London store. William Fortnum was a footman to Queen Anne. And one of the perks of his job was being allowed to keep the spent candles. The Royal Family insisted on new ones each night, which meant a lot of spare wax. Wax that he sold on for a decent profit. But it wasn't just the candles that kept Fortnum's coffers flowing. He also had a grocery sideline. And in 1707 he convinced his landlord, Hugh Mason, to go into business with him. So Fortnum met Mason. And they built their grocery as near as possible to the royal palace. Then, as now, St James's was the very centre of upscale, old-school society.

As Fortnum & Mason grew (helped by Fortnum's grandson, Charles, going into the household of Queen Charlotte, the wife of George III), so too did the British Empire. Wars raged, the map became steadily more pink, and the fortunes of Fortnum's grew. They supplied tea, wine and ale to the officers of Waterloo and Trafalgar alike. Queen Victoria sent out huge shipments of their famed beef tea to feed her armies during the Crimean War. And Robert Graves writes of Fortnum's hampers, filled with potted beef, Stilton and proper tea, arriving weekly in the World War I trenches. Winston Churchill was just one of many grateful recipients.

Yet Fortnum & Mason has never been content to live in the past. To respect it, sure, but never to become trapped in its amber grip. To stay still is to stagnate. They've always been innovators, from hampers and Scotch eggs to having their own beehives on the roof. With the Food and Drink Awards, they continually inspire (and reward) excellence in British food writing. And in 45 Jermyn St. they have a thoroughly modern restaurant that still values old-fashioned delight. Comfort, quality, the joys of a civilised long lunch.

This is the first official Fortnum & Mason cook book in over 300 years, the recipes a fusion of the classic and modern. But it is no mere coffee-table tome, destined to look good but gather dust – this is a book that should become splattered and worn with constant use, to be bent, bruised and loved. Like Fortnum & Mason itself, it aims to be timeless and practical, offering a taste of Britain with a resolutely global appetite. A keeper of British tradition and a curator of the world's greatest ingredients. The recipes, though, are all united by two things – their connection with Fortnum & Mason, and the fact that they taste damned fine too. So here's to the Grande Dame of Piccadilly. To good food, and cooking. And to the next 300 years.

NOIX GLACÉE
FORTNUM & MASON
REAL
TURTLE SOUP
FORTNUM & MASON
SELECTED
OX TONGUE
FORTNUM & MASON
Piccadilly, W.1
Famous for Quality
ENGLISH
GARDEN
PEAS
from
FORTNUM & MASON
LTD
PICCADILLY
W1
FORTNUM & MASON
Turkey
RODEL
BORDEAUX
FRANCE
SARDINES A L'HUILE D'OLIVE
"SEVEN
DELICACIES"
Asparagus
Spears
FORTNUM & MASON
JELLY

Ingredients

Good cooking starts with the best possible ingredients – a simple but fundamental Fortnum's philosophy. Listed here are some favourites, all of which will make the recipes in this book the best they can be.

Burford Brown eggs
The yolks are wonderfully creamy.

Butter
Fortnum's have some amazing butter, but one particular favourite is Abernethy butter, churned by hand in Ireland.

Honey
A great substitute for sugar, Fortnum's has an exquisite assortment of honeys.

Chardonnay vinegar
This delectably rounded vinegar will work wonders in any dressing.

25-month-aged Parmesan cheese
With a wonderfully salty and peppery flavour, this can be grated over carpaccio, asparagus or salads. Or simply eaten with honey.

Anchovies
Fortnum's use L'Escala anchovies – as a seasoning with lamb, in a salad, to boost the flavours of a dish, or served on toast.

Fortnum & Mason's Traditional Potted Stilton
From the last family-owned Stilton producer in the UK, this cheese can be made only with milk from the three 'Stilton counties' – Derbyshire, Nottinghamshire and Leicestershire.

Daphne's Welsh lamb
Produced by Daphne Tilley in Denbighshire, this is lamb as it's supposed to taste.

Fortnum's smoked salmon
The house cure comes from Severn & Wye in Gloucestershire. They use Var salmon (one of the most sustainable and fine-tasting farmed fish), gently smoked over oak. The result is a delicate, smoked salmon with languorous length and true depth of flavour.

Glenarm salt-aged beef
This beef is hand-selected from the Glenarm Estate in Northern Ireland. It is then dry-aged for 28–42 days in the producer's Himalayan salt chamber, a process that reduces moisture and intensifies the flavour.

Fortnum's Single Cask Madeira
This goes beautifully with most puddings. Once opened it will keep indefinitely. An ever-reliable store-cupboard ingredient.

Breakfast

'The English-speaking world divides roughly into two main camps – one camp swears by tea, the other coffee. Occasionally, each camp swears at the other. At Fortnum's, we maintain a strict neutrality. Here harmony reigns – for here you will find the best of both worlds'

Grilled Kippers with Lemon and Parsley Butter

After Edward VIII had abdicated, and was waiting, in exile, to marry Mrs Simpson at Château de Condé, he still craved a taste of home. So he had Fortnum's send down its Craster kippers (from Northumberland, with a strong oak smoke) every morning by plane. Anything to avoid that gloomy Continental breakfast.

Proper oak-smoked herrings are a classic British breakfast dish, although they seem to have fallen out of fashion in recent years. Why? All those fiddly bones? Perhaps. My mother reckons it's the smell, which tends to linger, but if you poach them, you'll have no such odorous issues. Anyway, the scent of grilling kippers is sublime.

As ever with such a simple, unfettered dish, quality is everything. A second-rate kipper is a mean and disconsolate thing. Fortnum's source theirs from Severn & Wye. The smoke is elegant and rather light. They're grilled, and served with a melting lump of good butter. Add a decent twist of pepper, and you have a breakfast fit for an (ex) king.

Serves 2

2 kippers
a little olive oil

For the lemon and parsley butter
50g softened unsalted butter
a small bunch of curly parsley, finely chopped
1 lemon

Put the butter into a small bowl and beat in the parsley. Add the zest of a quarter of the lemon, then cut the lemon in half, squeeze the juice from one half and beat that in too. Taste the butter and add more lemon zest or juice if you like.

Heat the grill and line the grill pan with foil. Place the kippers on it skin-side down and brush them lightly with olive oil. Grill for 6–8 minutes, then transfer to serving plates and top each kipper with a spoonful of the lemon and parsley butter. Serve with the remaining lemon half, cut in two, and some brown or granary toast.

Porridge

Porridge, stirred slowly, the old-fashioned way. Which means just water, real Scottish oats, salt and, if required, a splash of cream. Plus honey, the golden nectar that runs thick through Fortnum's veins. A simple dish, but one that has to be made just right. You sure don't want to annoy a Scotsman. In the eternal words of P. G. Wodehouse, 'It has never been hard to tell the difference between a Scotsman with a grievance and a ray of sunshine.'

Serves 4

1 litre water
a large pinch of salt
200g porridge oats

To serve
plenty of runny honey
double cream (optional)

Suggested toppings
golden raisins
sunflower seeds with ground cinnamon
sliced banana with maple syrup
blueberries with chia seeds

Bring the water and salt to the boil and whisk in the oats. Cook gently for 4–5 minutes, until the mixture has thickened and the oats are tender.

Ladle into 4 bowls and top with a generous swirl of honey and/or one of the toppings suggested. To make the porridge extra luxurious, add a good splash of double cream.

Boiled Egg and Soldiers

A boiled egg, I hear you cry? A boiled bloody egg? But everyone knows how to boil an egg. Get water to a rolling bubble, add egg, cook, and remove. Simple, right? Well, yes and no. We've all suffered the indignities of overcooked ovoids more suited to tennis than tucker. Or undercooked, where the white teeters on the translucent, and the yolk is still cold. But to Fortnum & Mason, perfection is all about just-firm white and oozing yolk, all the better for the buttered soldier's initial assault.

Traditionally, the bread was baked fresh on the premises, while the butter came up, in churns, from Somerset and Devon. It was there, thanks to all that lush grass, that the richest, sweetest and deepest yellow butter could be found. It was wrapped in lettuce leaves, to keep it cool, in the days before refrigeration.

As to instructions – the fresher the egg, the better. And please, never ever keep eggs in the fridge. There's no need and, if you do, plunging cold eggs straight into bubbling H_2O will cause them to crack.

---

1 Put the eggs into a pan of cold water.
2 Bring the water to the boil.
3 Turn off the heat and cover the pan.
4 Set your timer for the desired time:

3 minutes for really soft-boiled eggs
4 minutes for soft-boiled eggs
6 minutes for firm soft-boiled eggs
10 minutes for firm yet still creamy hard-boiled eggs
15 minutes for very firm hard-boiled eggs.

Serve with lavishly buttered toast soldiers. Plus a sprinkle of salt and pepper.

Brooding on
Easter
at FORTNUM'S
EB

Caviar Boiled Eggs

Caviar. 'As eaten by mermaids in cool grottos', according to the honeyed words of 'All The World's a Stage', a Fortnum & Mason Commentary from the early 1930s. These fearsomely expensive fish eggs have long been a favourite Fortnum's product, sourced from wild Volga sturgeon. Thanks, though, to rampant overfishing, the wild stuff is now illegal. Good. But farmed stuff is so fine these days that it would take a master to spot the difference. At 45 Jermyn St., a caviar trolley has been introduced. And its well-oiled wheels have barely stopped revolving. Here, with impeccable tableside theatrics, eggs are scrambled before your very eyes.

Serves 4

12 Burford Brown eggs
150ml double cream
70g unsalted butter, plus extra for buttering the toast
1 tablespoon chopped chives
20g Oscietra caviar
8 slices of sourdough bread, toasted
salt and freshly ground white pepper

Bring a large pan of water to a rapid boil and add 8 of the eggs. Simmer for 6 minutes. Remove the eggs from the pan and refresh under cold water. When they are just slightly warm, put the eggs in eggcups and cut the top off each one. Carefully remove the yolks with a teaspoon, mash them with a fork and set aside.

Crack the remaining 4 eggs into a bowl, add the double cream and some salt and pepper and whisk until combined.

Melt the butter in a heavy-based pan and add the beaten eggs. Cook gently, stirring, until they are softly scrambled. Remove from the heat and stir in the mashed egg yolks and the chopped chives. Fill the boiled eggs with the scrambled eggs and top with the caviar. Serve with the buttered, toasted sourdough.

Highland Scramble

At Fortnum's, the 45 Jermyn St. salmon cure is smoked on the roof, not far from the beehives. They also have a house cure, and organic and wild varieties too. Just add scrambled eggs, soft and buttery. Simple, but sublime.

Serves 4

80ml double cream
40g butter, plus extra for buttering the toast
salt and freshly ground white pepper
8 eggs, preferably Burford Browns, lightly beaten
250g smoked salmon
1 tablespoon chopped chives, to garnish
4 slices of sourdough bread, toasted
4 lemon wedges, to serve

Pour the double cream into a heavy-based pan and bring to the boil. Add the butter and heat until foamy. Season with salt and white pepper, then reduce the heat to low, add the beaten eggs and stir with a heatproof spatula until they are softly set. To prevent overcooking, it's best to take them off the heat a minute or so before they are done; they will continue to cook in the heat of the pan.

Arrange the smoked salmon in a nest on 4 serving plates. Put the scrambled eggs in the centre of each one and sprinkle with the chives. Serve accompanied by the buttered toast and the lemon wedges.

FORTNUM & MASON
PICCADILLY

Kedgeree with Smoked Haddock

A culinary love child of Empire, this Anglo-Indian dish has its roots in *khichri*, a deeply sub-continental mix of lentils, rice, herbs and spices. Bewhiskered brigadiers and very proper peers came back to Blighty with a taste for the dish, gradually adding fish, preferably smoked, in place of lentils, and a few boiled eggs for that true taste of Nanny's nursery. And so kedgeree was born.

Fortnum & Mason was always a spice pioneer, and was among the first British companies, around 1849, to mix its own curry powders. One of the Fortnum family was part of the East India Company. And Fortnum's even had a range of bottled curry sauces.

There's a whiff of cardamom and coriander in this recipe, plus coconut milk for the most gentle tropical allure. The eggs should be soft-boiled, and the curry spicing delicate rather than fierce.

Serves 4

2 tablespoons vegetable oil
2 shallots, finely diced
4 garlic cloves, crushed
4 cardamom pods
1 teaspoon coriander seeds
1 tablespoon medium curry powder
250g basmati rice
50g golden raisins
200ml coconut milk
250ml chicken stock
400g undyed smoked haddock
6 eggs
200ml crème fraîche
4 tablespoons chopped coriander
salt and freshly ground black pepper

Heat the vegetable oil in a heavy-based casserole, add the shallots and garlic, then cover and cook gently. Remove the cardamom seeds from the pods and lightly crush them in a pestle and mortar with the coriander seeds. Add them to the pan along with the curry powder and continue to cook for another 5–10 minutes, until the shallots are tender.

Rinse the rice in a sieve under the cold tap, then drain well and add to the pan, stirring to coat it with the spices. Add the raisins. Mix the coconut milk and stock together, add to the rice and bring to the boil. Cover the casserole tightly with a lid or aluminium foil and transfer to an oven heated to 180°C/Gas Mark 4. Cook for 20 minutes, until the liquid has been absorbed and the rice is tender. Remove from the oven and fluff the rice up gently with a fork. Season with salt and pepper.

While the rice is cooking, poach the smoked haddock. Put it into a large frying pan, cover with water and bring to a gentle simmer. It should be cooked through at this point; if not, turn it over and give it a minute longer. Remove from the pan, drain thoroughly and leave until cool enough to handle. Flake the flesh into large chunks, discarding the skin and any bones.

Soft-boil the eggs by adding them to a pan of boiling water and simmering for 4 minutes. Remove and cool under running water. When they are completely cold, shell the eggs, cut them into halves or quarters and set aside.

Put the crème fraîche into a pan, bring to a simmer, then add the cooked smoked haddock and cook gently for a couple of minutes to heat through. Gently fork the haddock and cream through the rice.

Serve in individual shallow bowls or in one large serving dish, garnished with the soft-boiled eggs and chopped coriander.

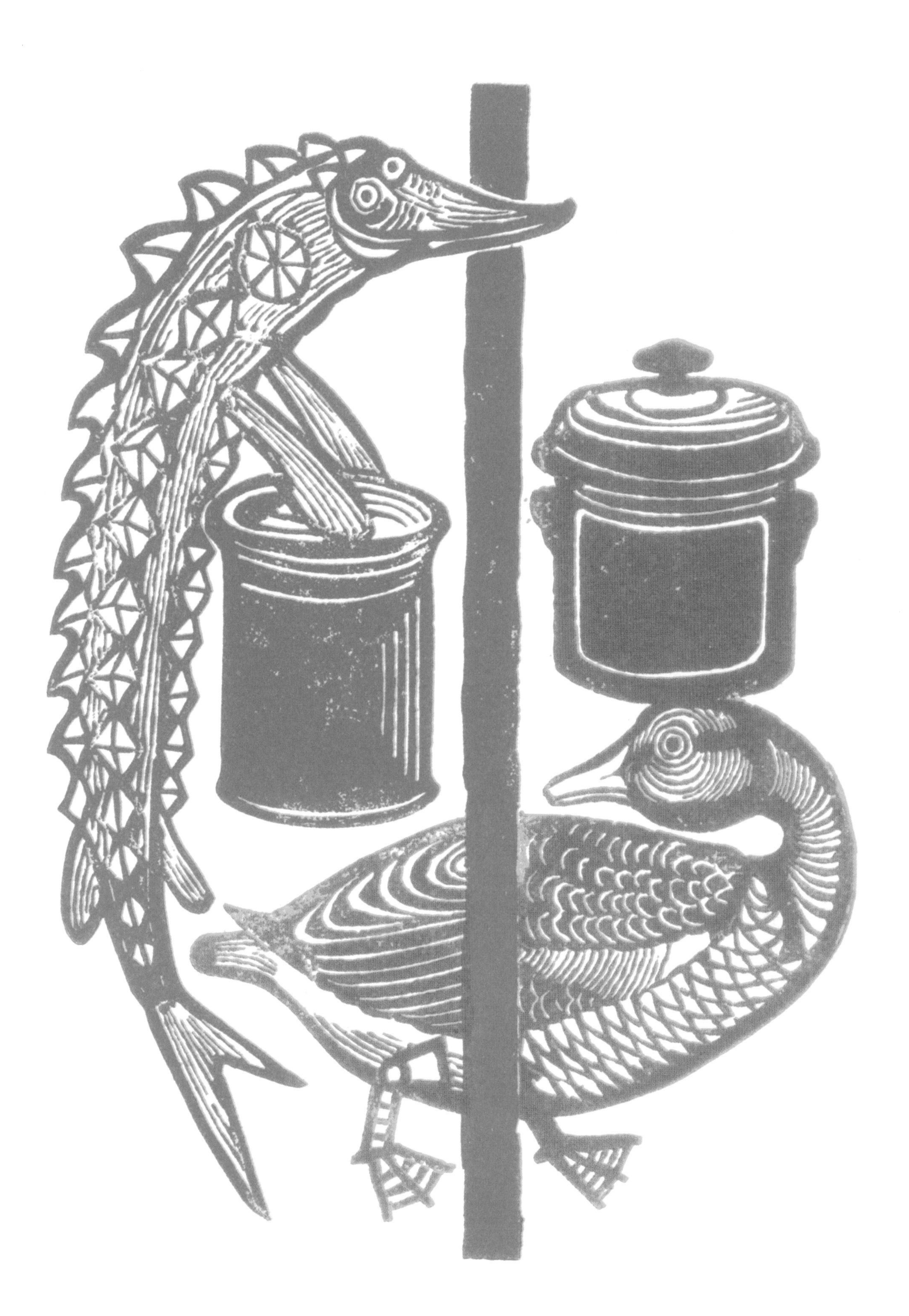

Toasted Crumpets with Marmite and Poached Burford Browns

This is a dish created for the opening of 45 Jermyn St. And there's some lively debate as to who actually invented this mightily British combination of butter, crumpet, Marmite and oozing egg. But whoever it was deserves a CBE for services to their country. Magnificent, and magnificently simple too.

Serves 2

50ml white wine vinegar
4 crumpets
4 Burford Brown eggs, at room temperature
unsalted butter
Marmite
ground black pepper

Fill a large saucepan with water and bring it to just under boiling point. Turn down to a simmer and add the vinegar.

Place the crumpets in a toaster; they should be double-toasted to give them a little crispness.

Crack each egg into a small cup (this makes it easier to poach 4 at the same time). With a slotted spoon, swirl the water around to create a whirlpool in the centre, then gently drop all the eggs into it. Turn the heat back up and, when it starts bubbling again, turn it back down to a low simmer. Poach the eggs for 3–4 minutes – they will rise to the surface when they are done. Remove them from the pan with the slotted spoon and put them on a wad of kitchen paper to soak up the excess water.

Spread the crumpets generously with butter, then spread with Marmite. Put them on 2 plates, top each one with a poached egg and sprinkle with a little ground black pepper.

Lobster Benedict

As if the classic eggs Benedict wasn't rich enough, the ham has been swapped for sweet chunks of lobster. Don't fear the Béarnaise sauce. Glass bowl. Gentle heat. Have faith. And make sure the lobster is a touch undercooked, as the warm sauce will bring it to soft succulence. As ever, organisation and preparation are everything. Get the ingredients in place before you start.

Serves 4

50ml white wine vinegar
8 very fresh eggs
20g unsalted butter
400g spinach
4 plain white muffins
350g cooked lobster, sliced
salt and freshly ground black pepper

For the Béarnaise sauce
200g unsalted butter
1 shallot, finely chopped
50ml white wine vinegar
50ml white wine
5 black peppercorns
4 sprigs of tarragon
3 large egg yolks
a pinch of cayenne pepper
2–3 teaspoons lemon juice

First make the Béarnaise sauce. Clarify the butter by melting it gently in a small pan, then pouring it into a jug, leaving the milky solids behind. Put the shallot, vinegar and wine into a small saucepan with the peppercorns and a sprig of tarragon and boil until reduced to about a tablespoon.

Strain into a large bowl. Set the bowl over a pan of gently simmering water, making sure the water doesn't touch the base of the bowl. Add the egg yolks and cook, whisking constantly with a balloon whisk, for about 3 minutes, until the mixture is pale and slightly thickened.

Reheat the melted butter in a microwave for a few seconds, if necessary; it should be lukewarm. Whisk it into the egg yolks a little at a time. As the sauce thickens and becomes more stable, you can add it faster. When you have a smooth, thick sauce, season with salt, cayenne pepper and lemon juice to taste. If the sauce is too thick, let it down with a little warm water (remember, this is a sauce, not mayonnaise). Chop the remaining tarragon sprigs and stir them in. Turn off the heat, but leave the bowl over the pan so the sauce keeps warm.

Next, poach the eggs. Fill a large saucepan with water and bring it to just under boiling point. Turn down to a simmer and add the vinegar. Crack 4 of the eggs into individual small cups (this makes it easier to poach 4 at the same time). With a slotted spoon, swirl the water around to create a whirlpool in the centre, then gently drop all 4 eggs into it. Turn the heat back up and, when it starts bubbling again, turn it back down to a low simmer. Poach the eggs for 3–4 minutes: they will rise to the surface when they are done. Remove them from the pan with the slotted spoon and put them on a wad of kitchen paper to soak up the excess water. Repeat with the 4 remaining eggs.

Heat the butter in a large frying pan, add the spinach and some salt and pepper and stir over a medium heat for 2–3 minutes, until the spinach has wilted. Transfer to a sieve and press out the excess liquid with the back of a wooden spoon.

Split and toast the muffins. Put 2 muffin halves on each serving plate and top with the spinach, followed by the lobster. Place the poached eggs on top and spoon over the Béarnaise sauce.

Baked Beans with Chorizo

Fortnum's use Heinz in this dish. Don't look so shocked. Fortnum & Mason were the first in Britain, back in 1886, to sell Mr Heinz's famed baked beans. And, in 2007, there was a special tin commissioned, clad in Fortnum's eau-de-nil, to commemorate the 300th anniversary of the store. This really is a dish to knock up in moments. A perfect lazy supper. Or weekend breakfast. With some shallots, butter, chorizo, parsley and Parmesan, this recipe takes the everyday and makes it great.

Serve with French bread. Diced streaky bacon makes a great alternative to the chorizo or, for vegetarians, you can substitute batons of fried courgette.

Serves 2

1 tablespoon olive oil
1 small shallot, finely diced
120g chorizo, cut into slices 5mm thick
1 x 415g tin of baked beans
30g butter, diced
1 tablespoon chopped parsley
20g Parmesan cheese, grated

Heat the olive oil in a frying pan, add the shallot and fry gently until softened. Add the chorizo and fry until caramelised and slightly crisp.

Heat the baked beans in a separate pan. Stir in the butter a few pieces at a time, then add the shallot and the oily juices from cooking the chorizo. Finally add the parsley and Parmesan cheese.

Serve the beans in shallow bowls with the chorizo on top.

Scrambling Prawns

This is a dish from the archives, hugely popular in the mid-50s as an hors d'oeuvre in the Outside Catering catalogue. Eggs scrambled with prawns, with a lobster bisque added for serious richness. You don't need tiger prawns, rather those smaller, more flavour-packed pink commas from the North Sea.

You do only need a little of the bisque for this recipe, but it freezes well and is perfect for shellfish soups and risottos. Use the shells left over from Lobster Benedict (see page 27) to make it.

Serves 4

25g unsalted butter
400g raw peeled Atlantic prawns
8 eggs, lightly beaten
2 tablespoons chopped chives
2 tablespoons chopped chervil
4 slices of white bread, crusts removed
3 tablespoons vegetable oil
salt and freshly ground black pepper

For the lobster bisque
about 500g lobster shells
4 tablespoons olive oil
1 carrot, diced
2 celery sticks, diced
1 leek, diced
1 onion, diced
4 sprigs of thyme
2 bay leaves
1 tablespoon tomato purée
50ml brandy
150ml white wine
50ml double cream

First make the lobster bisque. Break up the lobster shells into smaller pieces – or bash the thicker ones with a hammer. Put them into a roasting tin, drizzle over a little of the olive oil and place in an oven heated to 200°C/Gas Mark 6. Roast for 10–15 minutes. This step isn't essential but it will greatly improve the flavour of the bisque.

Meanwhile, heat the remaining oil in a large pan, add the carrot, celery, leek and onion and cook until softened but not coloured. Add the lobster shells, thyme, bay leaves and tomato purée. Cook, stirring, for a few minutes, until the tomato purée becomes a ruddy brown colour. Add the brandy, heat for a few seconds, then set it alight, standing well back. When the flames have died away, add the white wine and simmer until reduced by half. Pour in enough water to cover, bring to the boil and simmer for 1 hour, regularly skimming the froth from the surface. Strain through a fine sieve lined with a piece of muslin. Reheat gently, season with salt and pepper if necessary, and stir in the cream.

Heat the butter in a saucepan, add the prawns and some salt and sauté for 2–3 minutes, until the prawns are heated through but not coloured. Add 3 tablespoons of the lobster bisque and cook until slightly reduced. Add the beaten eggs and stir over a very low heat until softly scrambled. Be careful not to overcook them; they should be *baveuse* (soft). Stir in the herbs and check the seasoning.

Fry the bread in the vegetable oil until golden brown on both sides. Drain on kitchen paper, then place on 4 serving plates and top with the scrambling prawns. Drizzle 2 teaspoons of lobster bisque around each one.

Avocado with Toasted Sourdough Bread and Bloody Mary Sauce

Fortnum & Mason once had its very own team of plant hunters, scouring the globe for all things green, exciting and novel. Rather like Indiana Jones, with a pair of secateurs rather than a bullwhip. In fact, they were so respected that they even won a Gold Medal at the Great Exhibition in 1851.

This dish is hardly original, but is made piquant with Fortnum's own-blend vodka-spiked Bloody Mary sauce. Boozy but rather brilliant. You can always leave out the booze, or make double the amount of Bloody Mary, so you can sip one on the side. Perfect for starting the day with a bang.

Serves 2

2 ripe avocados
juice of ½ small lime
½ red chilli, deseeded and very finely diced
2 tablespoons chopped flat-leaf parsley
2 large slices of sourdough bread, toasted
salt and freshly ground black pepper

For the Bloody Mary sauce
50ml vodka
15ml lemon juice
½–1 teaspoon creamed horseradish sauce
4 dashes of Worcestershire sauce
4 drops of Tabasco sauce
75ml tomato juice
a pinch each of salt and pepper

To make the Bloody Mary sauce, mix all the ingredients together in a jug. Taste and adjust the seasonings if necessary, then set aside.

Cut the avocados in half, remove the stones, then peel and cut into small chunks. Transfer to a bowl and toss with the lime juice, chilli and salt and pepper to taste. Stir in the parsley.

Divide the mixture between 2 serving plates. Drizzle the Bloody Mary sauce over and around and serve immediately, accompanied by the sourdough toast.

Marmalade

Marmalade in the morning, someone once said, has the same effect upon the taste buds as a cold shower does on the body. It revives and refreshes, sharpening the senses with its exquisitely bitter bite. Fortnum's has an astonishing twenty-five varieties, ranging from the elegant and well behaved (Burlington Breakfast, with fine-cut peel and pale golden jelly) to the altogether more bold and forthright (Sir Nigel's Vintage Orange, created in the 1920s for actor-manager Sir Nigel Playfair. It's bitter, thick cut, dark and deep).

If these two extremes don't tempt, there's plenty of choice in between: Old Hunt, with medium-cut peel; Monarch, rich, regal and full-bodied; Dark Navy with Rum, for that slightly boozy kick; English Breakfast, infused with Royal Blend Tea. Even one with a chilli and ginger kick, the deliciously diabolical Lucifer's. And that's just the orange-based varieties. You can also find marmalade made with blood orange, pink grapefruit and lime.

Marmeleda was the Portuguese name for a solid quince paste, imported by the rich of England in the fifteenth century. Used as either medicine or a pudding dish, these solid marmalades (designed to be sliced and eaten as a sweetmeat) were also made from lemons and Seville oranges. Over time, the jellies became more soft and spreadable and eventually, some time in the eighteenth century, made their way on to our toast.

Fortnum's also has a close affiliation with the World's Original Marmalade Awards, for amateurs and artisans, based at Dalemain Mansion in Cumbria and started in 2006. Hundreds of jars are entered, and the annual 'Best in Show' is sold in store. Winners range from a traditional family recipe (Lord Henley in 2011), to the Radnor Preserves Smoky Campfire (2015's victor), a blend of orange, smoked salt, chilli flakes and maple syrup. A long way from the quince paste of old, but a worthy victor all the same.

And there are few things more British than toast, hot and thick, spread with cool butter and a blanket of marmalade. As a child, I couldn't bear the stuff. Too bitter by half, an unwanted taste of adulthood. But like olives, anchovies and pickled onions, marmalade gradually moves, with the passing of the years, from villain to steadfast ally. It's a fine ingredient in its own right too. Dribbled over steaming sponges, baked into teacakes and served up with sausages. That last combination is particularly sublime, where the sweet, salty and bitter all waltz together in a splendid breakfast dance.

I never quite mastered the art of making marmalade at home. The kitchen always ended up with every surface coated in sticky sugar, and the end result was either too runny or turgidly thick. Thank God, then, for Fortnum's marmalade. A style to suit every possible desire.

Marmalade-glazed Sausages

This may sound a little bizarre, but the match of sweet pork and bitter orange is one made in heaven. Fortnum & Mason used to supply Seville oranges (an advertisement was placed in *The Times* each January announcing the arrival of the new-season Sevilles) and sugar, but didn't make their own marmalade for the domestic market. They did, however, boil up batches for overseas from 1849, the perfect salve for those expats craving a taste of home.

By the 1920s, as technology began to burn as fierce as a sulphur flash, production was taken back in house and the famed range of Fortnum's marmalades began. There are a variety of different strengths. The Burlington is a nineteenth-century recipe, followed by the Old English Hunt, made for the Pytchley Hunt. But the most bitter and bold, with thick curls of peel, was created in 1926 for the great actor and manager Sir Nigel Playfair. It remains a bestseller to this day.

The best way to cook sausages is slow and low, over a gentle heat, turning them every now and again until the skin turns burnished and sticky.

Serves 2–3

1 Cumberland sausage ring
1 tablespoon vegetable oil
1 generous tablespoon dark, thick-cut marmalade
a knob of butter

Pass 2 long wooden skewers diagonally through the sausage ring to help it keep its shape during cooking.

Heat the oil in a frying pan, add the sausage and cook over a medium heat for about 25 minutes, until well browned on both sides and cooked through.

Pour off the excess oil, return the pan to the heat and stir in the marmalade, followed by the butter. Cook until the sausage is well coated, then put it on a plate, remove the skewers and spoon the remaining glaze over. Serve with extra marmalade, if you like.

Greek Yoghurt with Granola and Lime Marmalade

Home-made granola is key here, lots of fat nuts, plus flaked almonds, orange zest, demerara sugar, honey and golden syrup. A serious, fresh, grown-up granola, with that all-important balance of sweetness and citrus tang. Make it in large batches, as it will keep for 3–4 weeks in an airtight container. Add fresh or dried fruit at your discretion. And don't just stick to marmalade. Fruit compote, jam, milk and cream will all delight too.

Serves 4, with plenty of granola left for another day

300g Greek yoghurt
4 heaped tablespoons lime marmalade

For the granola
55g unsalted butter
60g honey
25g golden syrup
85g demerara sugar
1 teaspoon vanilla extract
25g hazelnuts, roughly chopped
75g pecan nuts, roughly chopped
35g pistachio nuts
50g flaked almonds
70g sunflower seeds
30g desiccated coconut
125g porridge oats
grated zest of 2 oranges

Put the butter, honey, golden syrup and demerara sugar into a pan and melt over a low heat. Remove from the heat and stir in the vanilla extract.

Combine all the dry ingredients in a bowl, add the orange zest and pour in the butter mixture. Mix until the dry ingredients are thoroughly coated. Spread the mixture out on a baking tray lined with baking parchment and place in an oven heated to 150°C/Gas Mark 2. Bake for 50–60 minutes, turning the mixture over every 15 minutes or so, until it is golden brown. Leave to cool and crisp up, then store in an airtight container.

To serve, spoon the Greek yoghurt into 4 glass dishes. Top with the lime marmalade and sprinkle a couple of generous spoonfuls of granola over it.

Scotch Pancakes with Marmalade

Made with buttermilk, these pancakes are soft and cloud-like. Pile 'em high. At Fortnum's, they are served with marmalade. But they're more traditionally served (in the US, at least) with bacon and maple syrup.

Makes about 20

250g plain flour
2 teaspoons bicarbonate of soda
2 teaspoons sugar
1 teaspoon salt
2 eggs
500ml buttermilk
100g unsalted butter, melted, plus extra for greasing
marmalade, to serve

Sift the flour, bicarbonate of soda, sugar and salt into a bowl and make a well in the centre. Add one egg and one egg yolk to the well and mix them in with a wooden spoon, drawing in the flour from the sides. Gradually beat in the buttermilk, followed by the butter. In a separate bowl, whisk the remaining egg white until stiff, then fold it into the mixture.

Place a large, heavy-based frying pan or a flat griddle pan over a medium heat and grease it lightly. Add a ladleful of the batter for each pancake – you should be able to cook 2 or 3 at a time. Cook for about 3 minutes, until the pancakes are golden brown underneath and are beginning to look dry around the edges on top. Flip them over to cook the other side. You can keep them warm in a low oven while you cook the rest, if necessary. Serve spread with marmalade – and with butter as well, if you like.

Marmalade-glazed Ham with Fried Duck Eggs

Ham meets Seville orange. Again. Not everyone has the time to glaze their own ham. But it's pretty easy. Simmer the joint, then slather sticky marmalade all over the surface (Sir Nigel's is perfect and has a bold tang) and bake. Duck eggs are rich and wonderful. But chicken eggs will do just fine. Serve with a spoonful of beetroot chutney, or any other chutney you like, on the side.

Serves 4, with ham leftovers

1 x 2kg ham joint
a few cloves to stud the ham
4 duck eggs
a good knob of butter, for frying
freshly ground black pepper

For the marmalade glaze
4 heaped tablespoons strong marmalade
½ teaspoon ground cinnamon
a pinch of ground cloves
25g dark soft brown sugar

Put the ham into a large pan, cover with cold water and bring to a simmer. Drain well, then cover with cold water again, bring to a simmer and cook gently for an hour. Drain again, then transfer the ham to a roasting tin and place it in an oven heated to 180°C/Gas Mark 4. Bake for 30 minutes. Meanwhile, mix together all the ingredients for the glaze.

Remove the ham from the oven and peel off the rind with a small sharp knife, leaving a good coating of fat. Score the fat in diamond shapes and stud each one with a clove. Coat the ham generously with the marmalade glaze, then return it to the oven and cook for 30 minutes, spooning the glaze in the tin over it from time to time, until it is burnished and golden.

Leave the ham to rest for about 10 minutes while you fry the duck eggs in the butter (if you keep the heat low, the whites will stay smooth and white). Carve the ham and serve each portion with a duck egg on top, sprinkled with a little freshly ground black pepper. Accompany with toasted sourdough or granary bread.

Morning Tea

'Such a tea as this makes the mind young with pleasure'

A combination as British as, well, Fortnum & Mason – tea and biscuits were always made to be together. Although baked at Fortnum's from the start, biscuits were originally big in the export trade. All that added sugar and fat was essential for those in search of the Northwest Passage. Or the speediest route up K2. The domestic market had no need (with the exception of a few delicate French-made fancies) to buy biscuits ready-made, as their cooks would do it for them. Of course.

But by the 1920s and 30s, biscuits were made fresh each day and sold alongside the fruits of the Chocolate and Cake Department. So people would come in for morning tea and biscuits. These days, biscuits are still hugely popular, ranging from Pistachio & Clotted Cream, to Dark Chocolate & Macadamia Nut to the mighty Chocolossus.

"THE ROARING FORTIES"
(of course, we ourselves never presumed to roar)

the most famous

TEA COUNTER

in the world

Ginger Biscuits

These babies have bite. Far more than your favourite shop-bought ginger nut. You really taste the fiery soul of this punchy root. Both candied and ground ginger are used, and demerara sugar adds its rich, redolent charms. The size may be small, but the flavour is immense.

Makes about 35

135g unsalted butter
135g golden syrup
300g plain flour
4 teaspoons baking powder
1 ½ teaspoons bicarbonate of soda
2 tablespoons ground ginger
105g demerara sugar
2–3 nuggets of candied ginger

Put the butter and golden syrup into a pan and heat gently until the butter has melted. Sift the flour, baking powder, bicarbonate of soda and ground ginger into a bowl. Stir in the demerara sugar, then make a well in the centre and grate in one of the pieces of candied ginger – either finely or coarsely, as you prefer. Add the melted butter and syrup to the well and stir to bring everything together into a dough.

Break off pieces of the dough approximately the size of a candied ginger nugget and roll each one into a ball. Place on baking sheets lined with baking parchment, spacing them about 6cm apart. Press each ball of dough to flatten it slightly.

Cut the remaining candied ginger into small dice and place a piece in the centre of each biscuit. Transfer to an oven heated to 160°C/Gas Mark 3 and bake for about 8 minutes, until golden. Leave to firm up on the baking sheet for a couple of minutes, then transfer to a wire rack to cool.

Note: once made, the cookie dough can be wrapped and frozen. Defrost and bake as required.

Florentine Biscuits

Despite them sounding resolutely Italian, you're actually more likely to find these sticky, lacy, candied-fruit creations in a French pâtisserie. 'An exceptionally delicious titbit', in the words of former Fortnum & Mason Executive Chef, Jean Conil.

These are slightly different from the classic Florentines, in that they sit on a pastry base. The honey caramel binding lies at their heart, with dried fruit and nuts, and should be made with a surfeit of double cream, while the final texture should be crisp, with a hint of the seductively chewy.

Makes 20

½ quantity of Sweet Pastry (see page 242)
50ml double cream
40g honey
40g unsalted butter
20g liquid glucose
115g caster sugar
85g mixed dried fruit, such as sultanas, diced apricots and quartered glacé cherries
120g flaked almonds
20g pistachio nuts, chopped

You will need a shallow baking tin approximately 30cm x 24cm. Roll out the pastry into a 4mm-thick rectangle and use to line the tin. Prick the pastry all over with a fork and chill for 30 minutes. Bake in an oven heated to 170°C/Gas Mark 4 for about 10 minutes, until very lightly coloured.

Meanwhile, put the cream, honey, butter, liquid glucose and caster sugar into a heavy-based pan and bring to the boil, stirring constantly. Remove from the heat and stir in the dried fruit and nuts. Pour the mixture carefully over the pastry base and spread it level. Return to the oven at 160°C/Gas Mark 3 and bake for 15–20 minutes, until golden.

Remove from the oven and cut into fingers when the topping has firmed up but is still warm.

Shortbread

Shortbread used to be made on the Fortnum's premises and is still a perennial bestseller. It's all about the butter, rather than hateful margarine, and that essential crumble. A tablespoon of porridge oats is added in this recipe for extra texture.

Makes 10

120g softened unsalted butter
70g caster sugar, plus extra for dusting
165g plain flour
15g porridge oats

Cream the butter and sugar together until light and fluffy. Sift in the flour, then mix in the oats and bring the mixture together to form a dough. Wrap in cling film and chill for 30 minutes.

Roll out the dough to about 1cm thick. Cut into rounds with a 6cm cutter and place on a baking sheet lined with baking parchment. Chill again for 30 minutes.

Place in an oven heated to 160°C/Gas Mark 3 and bake for 8–10 minutes, until very lightly coloured. Remove from the oven and sprinkle immediately with caster sugar, then leave to cool.

Teacakes

These are serious, fruity teacakes, toasted and slathered with butter and jam. This recipe makes pretty, petite mouthfuls. If you want more bulk, just shape into larger balls.

Makes 22 small teacakes

- 500g strong white flour
- 7g salt
- 50g caster sugar
- 15g milk powder
- 10g instant yeast
- 50g softened unsalted butter, diced
- 280ml water
- 180g currants
- 40g mixed peel

Put the flour, salt, sugar, milk powder and yeast into a large bowl. Add the butter and about three-quarters of the water and stir until well combined, adding the remaining water a little at a time until you have a fairly soft dough. Turn out on to a lightly floured board and knead for 8–10 minutes, until smooth and elastic. (Instead of doing all this by hand, you could mix and knead the dough in a freestanding electric mixer, if you have one.) Place in an oiled bowl, cover and leave for 1½–2 hours, until doubled in size.

Knock back the dough and turn it out on to a lightly floured work surface again. Add the currants and mixed peel and work them in well – it may look like too much at first but the dough will be able to hold it all if you persist. Divide the dough into 22 pieces – you can weigh them for accuracy if you want them all to be exactly the same size. Shape each one into a ball, rotating it under your hand on the work surface until smooth.

Place the balls of dough on 2 baking sheets lined with baking parchment, spacing them a few centimetres apart, and flatten slightly with your hand. Cover loosely with cling film or a tea towel and leave to prove until the teacakes have almost doubled in size.

Place in an oven heated to 200°C/Gas Mark 6 and bake for about 10 minutes, until golden. Leave the teacakes to cool, then split and toast them – or eat untoasted, if you prefer. Serve with lots of butter and jam.

Peanut Hob Biscuits

Oats, golden syrup and peanut butter – chunky, of course. Proper biscuits, and rather light too. Plus the children love making them, as the recipe is blissfully simple. Try to use the best peanut butter you can find, as it will improve the result no end. You could even spread them with a little strawberry jam, for a British take on peanut butter and jelly.

Makes 25–30

125g strong white flour
65g light soft brown sugar
125g rolled oats
½ teaspoon salt
125g unsalted butter
125g golden syrup
¼ teaspoon bicarbonate of soda
25ml water
60g chunky peanut butter

Put the flour, sugar, oats and salt into a bowl and stir to combine. Melt the butter and golden syrup together. Mix the bicarbonate of soda with the water, add it to the melted butter and golden syrup and mix well. Stir into the dry ingredients, then add the peanut butter and mix until combined into a dough. Leave to cool.

Shape heaped teaspoons of the mixture into balls and place them on baking sheets lined with baking parchment, spacing them well apart. Flatten the balls slightly. Place in an oven heated to 160°C/Gas Mark 3 and bake for 10–12 minutes, until golden brown. Leave the biscuits on the baking sheets for a few minutes, then transfer to a wire rack to cool.

Any excess mixture can be rolled into a cylindrical shape, wrapped in cling film and frozen. When you want to bake, remove the dough from the freezer, leave to defrost, slice and bake as above.

Garibaldi Biscuits

Better known to generations of children as the 'squashed fly', these slender biscuits are named after the great unifying Italian general. He even made a visit to South Shields in 1854, and the first recorded recipe is in 1861, where it was manufactured by Peek Freans. These are rather different from the packet version, though, more crisp, and less chewy and dense. Plus a wonderful scent of orange too. For best results, roll as thin as you dare.

Makes 35–40

250g plain flour
1½ teaspoons baking powder
a pinch of salt
60g unsalted butter, diced
40g light soft brown sugar
60ml orange juice
20ml water
1 egg, lightly beaten
250g raisins, chopped
1 egg white, lightly beaten
granulated golden sugar

Sift the flour, baking powder and salt into a bowl and rub in the butter with your fingertips until the mixture resembles fine crumbs. Stir in the sugar. Add the orange juice and water and mix to a fairly soft dough. Wrap in cling film and chill for 30 minutes or so.

On a lightly floured surface, roll the dough out into a rectangle 3–4mm thick. Brush half of it with the beaten egg and sprinkle the chopped raisins on top. Fold the other half of the pastry over the raisin-covered side, pressing the edges together to seal. Roll out to 3–4mm thick again.

Prick the dough all over with a fork, brush with the egg white and sprinkle with granulated golden sugar. Cut into fingers and transfer to a baking sheet lined with baking parchment (you may need more than one sheet). Place in an oven heated to 180°C/Gas Mark 4 and bake for about 8 minutes, until golden.

Crumpets

Bought crumpets are lovely but they are also very easy, and quick to make. You will need some crumpet or chef's rings.

Makes 12

275ml milk
1 teaspoon caster sugar
250g strong white flour
1 tablespoon dried yeast
½ teaspoon bicarbonate of soda
1 teaspoon salt
butter, for frying and serving

Put the milk and 55ml water into a saucepan, warm over a gentle heat, then stir in the sugar. Put the flour into a bowl and stir in the yeast. Pour in the warm milk and stir together until smooth. Cover the bowl with a tea towel and leave in a warm place until the batter is frothy and full of bubbles. This can take anything from 20 minutes to a couple of hours.

Mix the bicarbonate of soda and salt with about 50ml warm water (you may need a little more). Gradually beat this into the batter until it is smooth.

Butter the insides of the crumpet rings. Heat a large frying pan or flat griddle and grease with a little butter. Put a couple of rings into the pan and add a tablespoon of batter to each one. Cook for 4–5 minutes, until bubbles, then holes, appear on the surface. Turn the crumpets over to cook the tops (this will take about a minute), then remove them and cook the rest of the batter in the same way.

Serve warm with lots of butter or one of the suggested toppings.

Crumpet Toppings

Hot, chewy and dripping with butter, the crumpet is a thing of gentle majesty. Especially when topped with mango chutney butter or honeyed cream cheese. A welcome elevenses, sure, but a snack that suits any whim, or time of the day.

Honey and Cream Cheese

1 tablespoon cream cheese
1 teaspoon good-quality honey
a few black sesame seeds

Mix the cream cheese and honey together and spread on a hot toasted crumpet. Add a sprinkling of black sesame seeds.

Marmalade and Lemon Curd

2 teaspoons marmalade
2 teaspoons lemon curd

Mix the marmalade and lemon curd together and spread on a hot toasted crumpet.

Mango Chutney Butter

2 teaspoons softened butter
2 teaspoons mango chutney
a pinch of chia seeds

Mix the butter and mango chutney together and spread on a hot toasted crumpet. Sprinkle with the chia seeds.

Seed Cake

An old-fashioned English classic, flavoured with ground almonds and a handful of caraway seeds. It may sound a little dull, but believe me, it ain't. Don't overdo the caraway, though, as it can tend to overwhelm any subtle notes. Topped with a golden crunch, this cake goes well with tea or coffee. Even better with a mid-morning glass of Madeira.

You can also add chopped peel if so desired. Fortnum's has a huge range of whole candied fruit, which is superior to anything ready-cut from a supermarket.

Makes 1 large loaf

175g softened unsalted butter
175g caster sugar
3 large eggs, lightly beaten
250g self-raising flour
2 dessertspoons ground almonds
1 dessertspoon caraway seeds
40ml milk

For the topping
1 tablespoon flaked almonds, roughly crushed
1 tablespoon demerara sugar
1 tablespoon rolled oats

Beat the butter and sugar together until light and fluffy. Beat in the eggs a little at a time, then fold in the flour, followed by the ground almonds and caraway seeds. Finally fold in the milk.

Transfer the mixture to a greased and lined 900g loaf tin. Mix together all the topping ingredients and sprinkle them over the cake. Place in an oven heated to 160°C/Gas Mark 3 and bake for 40–45 minutes, until the cake is well risen and golden brown and a skewer inserted into the centre comes out clean. Leave the cake to cool in the tin for about 10 minutes, then turn out on to a wire rack to cool completely.

Tea

Tea. Perhaps the most iconic of the Fortnum & Mason offerings, and certainly one of the first. And as important as William Fortnum's candle wax, upon which the empire was built. Because there can be no shop on earth where the leaves of *Camellia sinensis* (to address it in the most formal of terms) are treated with such reverence, and found in such great variety.

From the well-known blends (and the art of the blend, from Breakfast to Royal, is one for which Fortnum's has long been famed), through the classic geographical areas (Assam, Darjeeling, Ceylon, Yunnan), the specialist (Gyokuro, perhaps Japan's finest tea), and incredibly rare Single Estate beauties (100-Year-Old Tree, made from one of the oldest tea bushes in the Fenghuang Mountains), there are nearly 150 varieties in store at any one time. In 2015, an astonishing 230,000 pots were sold in the Diamond Jubilee Tea Salon and Gallery alone.

The ground floor is a temple to the dried leaf, a grand bazaar of tea caddies that brings together the finest varieties from India, China, Sri Lanka, Japan, Kenya, Taiwan, Nepal and even the UK. And these blessed leaves are inextricably entwined with the shop's long and lustrous history. Okay, so the first imported variety – way back in 1712 – was the Chinese Black Bohea, made from inferior stalk, rather than the all-important leaf. But at 25 shillings a pound (about £100 in today's money) it was an expensive brew, kept locked away in a tea caddy, way out of the reach of normal folk. Indeed, back then, tea was very much an aristocratic tipple.

Now, of course, it's not only gloriously democratic but, after water, the most widely consumed drink in the world. As ever, though, at Fortnum & Mason, quality and consistency are paramount. And speaking to their buyers is like being whisked away to some far-off, romantic land, one filled with mist-shrouded plantations, secret gardens and tiny, family-run factories where the leaves are still roasted by hand. Terroir (climate, soil and geomorphology) is as important in growing tea as it is with grapes. And the relationship between Fortnum's tea buyer and supplier often stretches back many generations, bonded by trust, respect, and more than a few sundowners too. It means that Fortnum's has a direct link with the growers, choosing the very finest leaves. These close relationships ensure quality, consistency and all-important provenance.

India (Assam and Darjeeling), Ceylon (Sri Lanka) and China are still the main suppliers. And the leaves are turned into black, green, oolong or white tea, depending on how they are processed. It all starts with the first 'invoice', the very first taste of the crop of the year. It's an indication of how the season is going to turn out, and one that gets Fortnum's buzzing with caffeinated excitement. Much of the art is in the picking. Buyers look at how well the leaf has been twisted, and how much tip (where the most refined flavour resides) is left. As a tea-plucker, it's much quicker and easier to pick the huge, dark, coarse leaves. But Fortnum's insist on the very top of the plant, just two leaves and a bud (though there are always exceptions to the rule where the buds are not desired, depending on the style of tea). It is, of course, a markedly more skilled, and time-consuming task. But all-important when it comes to the final taste.

Once the best leaves and buds have been picked, they begin to wilt and oxidise. And need to be rolled and dried. Sharpish. The level of oxidation is key to the tea: too little, and the flavour is wan and underdeveloped; too much, and the taste will be stewed and over-fruity. Every single stage of the process, from picking to brewing, must be done just right to create that perfect cup of tea. Including the art of the blend, where the Fortnum's buyers and tasters mix a variety of leaves (and assorted flavour additions) to produce a cup of something wonderful. Experience is key, and knowledge too, in creating something that will remain consistently fine for the entire year. Which is why the Fortnum & Mason pot of tea, in whatever variety you choose, is no mere cuppa. Rather it's the distillation of Fortnum's obsession, and the purest expression of the tea-grower's art.

F&M

The Art of Tea

All this hard work, dedication and expertise means nothing if the tea is made with slapdash indifference. There is a true art to the brew. Loose leaf will always give the better pot. The leaves are whole and unbroken, expanding as they steep, releasing all those fragrant oils, flavours and aromas. In short, they stretch to release their full potential. Which is not to say that the Fortnum's tea bags are in any way comparable to the low-grade, mass-market, dusty 'floor sweepings', with their aggressive tannins and one-note tang. Fortnum's tea bags also contain whole leaf, and of a high quality too. But for tea purists, it's always loose over bag.

You should make it your way. If you like your tea with milk and sugar, fine. But there are certain teas (Afternoon Blend, for example) that are best drunk without milk so that you can appreciate their refreshing, brisk nature.

Here is the Fortnum & Mason guide to making a flawless pot.

1

Always make a pot of tea with fresh water. When it's been boiled once, it loses its oxygen. And its zing. Flat, stagnant water does not make for a good pot.

2

Warm up your teapot. Most black teas (e.g. Royal Blend) need water at boiling point to release all their flavours. When hot water hits cold porcelain, the temperature drops and you won't get to appreciate all the joy contained within the leaves.

3

Brew most teas for 4 to 5 minutes; 1 to 3 minutes with some of the greens. A common British problem is not brewing for long enough. The buyers wince when they see a tea bag dipped in the water for 10 seconds, then taken out. The result is little more than caramel-coloured hot water, and you'll lose all that lovely flavour they've worked so hard to create.

4

But don't over-brew. If the leaves spend too much time in the hot water, they'll stew, resulting in a bitter, over-strong cuppa.

5

If you do wish to add milk, please make sure this is done after the tea has fully brewed in the water. We recommend that milk is added to the cup first, then your freshly, fully brewed tea is poured into the milk. This gradually heats the milk rather than 'shocking' it. It also helps to protect your best china from cracking.

What tea to drink, when

Morning

You need something with a little bit of oomph and muscle, to shake you from your early-morning fuzz. 100% Assam is always a good starter, as it is strong and can take milk. Or Royal Blend, made with a splash of milk, as it's equally strong, bright and possesses that all-important morning kick. It's made with Assam and low-grown Ceylon. Assam gives a malty rich character, with Ceylon chosen for a full-bodied, caramelesque taste too.

Afternoon

As the day moves on, the need for the morning blast passes and we move into the more delicate and refined afternoon styles, such as Fortnum's Afternoon Blend, which contains Ceylon, for its refreshing, brisk nature. Or Earl Grey, which can be taken with the tiniest drop of milk. Fortnum's keep the bergamot on a tight lead, as it can dominate the tea and stamp all over any delicate notes. Another classic is the Chinese Lapsang Souchong, black and smoky. Smoky Earl Grey – which has a touch of Lapsang Souchong – is in fact Fortnum's original Earl Grey blend.

Dinner

A Rock Oolong from China, with its toasty, roasted notes, goes beautifully with beef, while a Japanese Gyokuro is clean and savoury and elegantly complements Asian noodles, sushi and fish. After dinner, Jasmine Pearls cleanse the palate.

Fortnum's Favourites

Wake up to a cup of Royal Blend – it's rich, thick and satisfying. Royal Blend with toast and marmalade is one of life's simple pleasures.

Mid-morning calls for a caffeine top-up. Rose Pouchong tea is the first choice, delicate and floral – such a delectable way to keep hydrated.

Afternoon tea calls for three options – if in need of a treat, the choice is either a refreshing first-flush Darjeeling, or a cup of Anji Baicha Green Tea (a really special treat). Or simply a cup of loose-leaf Earl Grey. Nothing is more comforting.

Lunch

'... who flew a helicopter from Battersea to Luton last Friday? Check non-commercial air traffic out of Luton, check any North Sea islands for hire. Look for one with a gazebo. And follow the Fortnum's hamper: who ordered it, paid for it, delivered it. Get me the invoice. *Smoked Salmon for Congo Lovers*. I love it'

John le Carré, *The Mission Song*

Fish and Chips with Minted Peas

What can I say . . . a British classic, a golden-battered, Rule-Britannia-warbling stalwart that is as iconically British as roast beef, plum pudding and a surfeit of beer. It has always been on the Fortnum's menu, and is an eternal bestseller. Here, it's breadcrumbed, with Japanese panko, rather than battered, which gives a really crisp coating to the fish. Light, too.

The chips, fat and proud, should be double-cooked, for a crisp exterior and soft centre. Always make sure you use fresh, clean oil. You can prepare everything in advance up to the last frying.

Oh, and the dish is not John Bull British in origin, as you might have believed, rather a happy marriage of Jewish (Ashkenazi immigrants would sell cold fried fish on the streets of London) and French (who invented the chip as we know it). But worry not, flag wavers . . . it was the British who put the two together. And the Brits who still worship at its burnished, lightly vinegared feet.

Serves 4

900g floury potatoes, preferably Maris Piper
vegetable oil, for deep-frying
20g plain flour
finely grated zest of ½ lemon
2 eggs, lightly beaten
100g breadcrumbs, preferably Japanese panko crumbs
4 x 180g pieces of haddock fillet, skinned and pin-boned
sea salt and freshly ground black pepper

For the tartare sauce
100g good-quality mayonnaise
1 small shallot, finely chopped
2 tablespoons chopped flat-leaf parsley
20g cornichons, finely chopped
20g capers

For the minted peas
300g frozen peas
60g unsalted butter
leaves from a sprig of mint, finely chopped

Peel the potatoes and cut them into chips 12mm thick. Place in a steamer in a single layer (you'll probably have to cook them in several batches; alternatively you can par-boil them) and steam for 8 minutes; they should just be beginning to soften. Drain well and leave to cool.

Heat the vegetable oil to 110°C in a deep-fat fryer or a large, deep saucepan (if using a saucepan, don't fill it more than a third full). Fry the chips in batches for 6–8 minutes, until they are soft but not coloured. Drain well on kitchen paper and set aside. (They can be prepared up to this stage several hours in advance.)

Mix together all the ingredients for the tartare sauce and set aside.

For the minted peas, cook the peas in boiling salted water until tender, then drain well. Refresh in iced water and drain again. Heat thoroughly in a pan with the butter, then blitz briefly with a hand blender to make a chunky mixture. Stir in the mint and season to taste.

Next prepare the fish. Put the flour into a shallow dish and mix it with the lemon zest and some salt and pepper. Put the beaten eggs into another dish and the breadcrumbs into a third. Pat the fish dry and coat each piece first with the flour, then with the egg and finally with the breadcrumbs, patting them on to give an even coating.

Heat the oil again – this time to 160°C. Lower the fish into the oil, cooking 2 pieces at a time so as not to overcrowd the pan. Fry for about 6 minutes, until golden brown, then drain on kitchen paper while you finish off the chips.

Raise the temperature of the oil to 190°C. Fry the chips in batches until they are crisp and golden brown, draining them on kitchen paper and seasoning with salt as they are done.

Reheat the peas briefly, if necessary. Serve the fish and chips accompanied by the tartare sauce and minted peas.

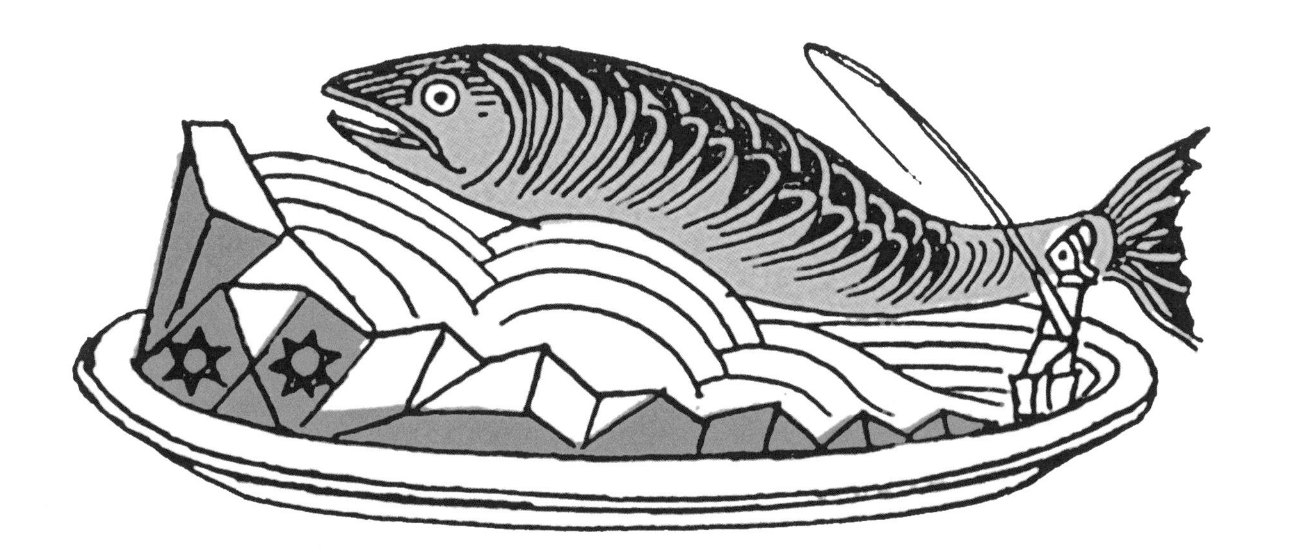

Fish Pie

Now this is a serious fish pie, with smoked haddock, salmon and cod at its heart. Plus prawns and green beans, for added texture. Feel free to substitute some of the ingredients (just replace with the same amount of a different fish). Or even swap scallops for prawns. The Parmesan crust adds yet another layer of richness. In short, a piscine feast to impress Neptune. Or any hungry friends. The recipe is for individual pies, but it's just as easy to bake it in a big dish too.

Serves 4

900g floury potatoes, such as Desiree, peeled and cut into chunks
110g unsalted butter
600ml whole milk, plus a little extra for the mash, if needed
200g undyed smoked haddock
2 bay leaves
100g salmon fillet, skinned and diced
100g cod fillet, skinned and diced
100g fine green beans, cut in half
50g plain flour
5 tablespoons chopped flat-leaf parsley
200g cooked Atlantic prawns
40g Parmesan cheese, freshly grated
salt and freshly ground black pepper

Cook the potatoes in a large pan of boiling salted water until tender. Drain well and mash over a low heat; this helps any excess water in the potatoes steam away. Beat in 50g of the butter and season well, adding a splash of milk if the mash is too stiff.

Poach the smoked haddock by putting it in a pan with the milk and bay leaves and bringing to a gentle simmer. It should be cooked through at this point; if not, turn it over and give it a minute longer. Remove the fish from the pan and flake the flesh into chunks, discarding the skin and any bones. Reserve the milk.

Steam the diced salmon and cod for 4–5 minutes, until just cooked through. Cook the green beans in a pan of boiling salted water for 4 minutes, until tender, then drain and refresh in cold water (this helps preserve their bright colour).

Meanwhile, melt the remaining butter in a pan and stir in the flour to form a roux. Cook for 1–2 minutes over a gentle heat. Strain the warm milk into a jug and gradually add it to the roux, stirring constantly, until you have a smooth sauce. Simmer for a few minutes, then season to taste and stir in the chopped parsley.

Pour a little of the sauce into 4 individual pie dishes (or one large dish). Divide the fish, beans and prawns between them and cover with the rest of the sauce. Allow to cool so that the sauce sets. Top with the mashed potato. Sprinkle with the Parmesan cheese and bake in an oven heated to 180°C/Gas Mark 4 for about 20 minutes, until golden brown and thoroughly heated through.

Steak Tartare

The St James's restaurant opened in 1955, up on the fourth floor, next door to the Antiques Department. It was a slightly more formal, serious older sister to the Fountain, popular with the *grandes dames* of the theatre, and the grand ladies who liked to lunch. Later on, Terence Stamp had his favourite table, complete with his own waitress, Margaret. The menu was huge, the atmosphere suitably stately.

Steak tartare was a great favourite. The best fillet should be used, seared first to remove any lingering bugs, then the cooked bits discarded. But at home, that's not strictly necessary. Hand chopping is key, not just to ensure that every errant piece of sinew is removed, but to produce a texture that is quite impossible to achieve via a machine. As to the extras, all those cornichons and capers add bite, along with the unctuous slick of egg yolk and a good dash of Worcestershire sauce and Tabasco. But this is another dish that must be adapted to taste.

Serves 2

300g beef fillet
40g tomato ketchup
1 teaspoon Dijon mustard
½ teaspoon Worcestershire sauce
5 drops of Tabasco sauce
20g cornichons, diced
15g capers
2 small shallots, very finely diced
2 tablespoons coarsely chopped flat-leaf parsley
2 very fresh organic egg yolks
sea salt and freshly ground black pepper
toasted sourdough bread, to serve

Heat a heavy-based frying pan until it is very hot, then add the beef fillet and sear it briefly all over, ensuring that every surface comes into contact with the pan. Remove from the pan and leave to cool, then chill. Slice off all the sealed meat, leaving just the raw meat. (This process helps ensure that the meat is safe to eat.) Using a very sharp knife, dice the beef as finely as possible – aim for dice of roughly 2mm. Scrape off and discard any sinew as you go.

Put the beef into a bowl. Mix together the tomato ketchup, mustard, Worcestershire sauce and Tabasco and combine them with the beef. Fold in the cornichons, capers, shallots and parsley and season to taste.

Put a 10cm ring mould on a serving plate and press half the tartare mixture into it. Remove the ring and repeat on a second plate with the remaining mixture. Make a small dip in the centre of each portion (you could use a washed egg shell for this) and add an egg yolk to it. Sprinkle a pinch of sea salt on top of the egg yolks, then serve with toasted sourdough bread.

Dressed Salmon

A hugely popular dish when it came to Outside Catering, and a British summer classic. Back in the early twentieth century, there was only Scottish wild salmon. Lucky them. Now, though, these mighty fish are rather a rarity, with a price to match. But if you can get your hands on this handsome, firm-fleshed beast, the dish will really sing. You do need a fish kettle, or a large roasting tin at the very least. Poach in a gently simmering court-bouillon (for yet another layer of flavour), so the fish is just opaque. Overcooked salmon is a sin. Let it cool down in the water.

Jean Conil, that great Fortnum's Executive Chef of the 1950s, was a huge fan, although the decoration (over-dressed, over-piped, with cucumber scales and perched upon a huge block of carved ice) could be a little excessive for the home cook. But this is a showstopper of an old-fashioned dish. And a spectacle, in every way.

Serves 8–10

1 side of salmon, weighing 1–1.5kg, pin-boned

For the court-bouillon
2 onions, chopped
1 leek, chopped
4 celery stalks, chopped
2 bay leaves
2 teaspoons white peppercorns
200ml white wine
100ml white wine vinegar
1 lemon, cut in half
40g salt
4 litres water

For the garnish
200g crayfish tails
4 tablespoons Marie Rose sauce (see page 84)
½ cucumber, thinly sliced
coriander cress or watercress

Put all the ingredients for the court-bouillon into a fish kettle or large roasting tin and gently lower the salmon into the water. Put it on the hob over a medium heat. It's really important not to let the water boil; you just need to bring it to a very light simmer. This should take about 20 minutes, and as the water warms it will poach the salmon. When the water reaches a simmer, check that the flesh of the fish is firm to the touch. If not, give it a couple of minutes longer. Otherwise, remove the fish kettle from the heat and leave the salmon to cool in the water for 20–30 minutes. Transfer it carefully to a board and leave to cool completely.

For the garnish, mix the crayfish and Marie Rose sauce together. Arrange them down the centre of the salmon, then make a border of cucumber slices all round the fish. Decorate with a few sprigs of coriander cress or watercress.

Smoked Haddock Fishcakes with Caper Butter Sauce

A staple from The Diamond Jubilee Tea Salon. And one with as much fish as potato. You need the best smoked haddock you can buy – none of that garish yellow stuff, please. The caper butter sauce cuts through the comforting heft of the fishcakes, adding sharpness and zing. The best capers are from Italy (in particular, the island of Pantelleria), and are packed in salt. Oh, and baking the potatoes for the mash ensures a dry, light, very fluffy result.

Serves 4

2 large baking potatoes (about 500g in total)
25g softened unsalted butter
2 shallots, finely chopped
500g undyed smoked haddock fillet
3 tablespoons white wine
3 tablespoons chopped curly parsley
50g plain flour
1 egg, lightly beaten with 4 tablespoons milk
100g breadcrumbs, preferably Japanese panko crumbs
a knob of butter and 1 tablespoon vegetable oil, for frying
salt and freshly ground black pepper
lemon wedges, to serve

For the caper butter sauce
600ml fish stock
1 shallot, chopped
50ml Noilly Prat vermouth
75ml double cream
75g cold unsalted butter, diced
2 teaspoons lemon juice
25g capers
1 tablespoon chopped parsley

Wrap the potatoes individually in foil and bake in an oven heated to 200°C/Gas Mark 6 for about an hour. When they are tender, leave until cool enough to handle, then cut them in half and scoop out the flesh into a large bowl, mashing it well.

Smear the soft butter over a large piece of foil and scatter over the shallots. Put the haddock on top, season and pull up the sides of the foil. Pour the white wine over the fish, then wrap the fish up loosely in the foil, making sure it is well sealed. Bake at 180°C/Gas Mark 4 for about 8 minutes. Remove from the oven, drain the fish and leave to cool.

Flake the fish, discarding the skin and any bones. Mix with the potato and chopped parsley and check the seasoning. Roll the mixture into 8 balls and press the top of each one with a spatula to flatten it. Shape into neat cylinders about 5cm thick.

Put the flour into a shallow dish, the egg and milk into another and breadcrumbs into a third. Coat the fishcakes lightly with flour, then with egg and finally coat evenly with breadcrumbs. They can be chilled until you are ready to cook them.

To make the sauce, boil the fish stock until reduced by about two-thirds. Add the shallot and Noilly Prat and boil until reduced by half. Add the cream and let the mixture reduce by half again, then gradually whisk in the butter until you have a smooth, glossy sauce. Stir in the lemon juice, capers and parsley and season to taste. Keep warm.

To cook the fishcakes, heat the butter and oil in a large frying pan, add the fishcakes and fry over a medium heat until golden brown on both sides. Transfer to an oven heated to 180°C/Gas Mark 4 and cook for 6–8 minutes, until piping hot right through. Serve with the sauce and lemon wedges.

Potted Rabbit with Cornichons

Before refrigeration turned food preservation from necessity to personal preference, potting (spiced meat or fish, covered with clarified butter) not only made your food last longer, but added to the flavour too. And rabbit was a Fortnum's favourite, tinned and potted for export. In the UK, most customers (or their gamekeepers) shot their own. During the war, rabbits were classified as vermin, and therefore off ration.

Farmed rabbit has more fat, but less flavour. Go with wild if you can. If you can't find rabbit legs you can use duck instead. Which would make it potted duck. Or chicken legs. It will keep for a week or so in the fridge.

Serves 6

4 rabbit legs
600g duck fat
1 carrot, peeled and cut lengthwise into quarters
3 garlic cloves, peeled
a sprig of rosemary
a bunch of parsley, chopped

For the salt cure
200g flaky sea salt, such as Maldon
3 garlic cloves, peeled
1 teaspoon black peppercorns
1 tablespoon coriander seeds
1 tablespoon fennel seeds
a bunch of thyme
1 bay leaf

To serve
6 slices of sourdough bread, toasted
a small jar of cornichons

Roughly blitz all the cure ingredients in a food processor. Put the rabbit legs into a dish that will hold them in a single layer, cover with the salt mix, then cover the dish with cling film. Leave to marinate in the fridge for 24 hours.

The next day, rinse the salt mix off the rabbit legs and pat them dry. Melt the duck fat in a large casserole. Add the carrot, garlic, rosemary and rabbit legs. Make sure the legs are covered with the fat, then bring to a simmer. Cut out a circle of baking parchment the same diameter as the casserole and put it on top of the mixture. Place a lid on the casserole and cook in an oven heated to 150°C/Gas Mark 2 for about 2 hours, until the meat comes off the bone easily. Remove from the oven and leave the legs in the fat until they are cool enough to handle.

Remove the carrot and garlic from the fat and pulse in a food processor. Take out the rabbit legs and pick off all the meat from the bones, discarding the skin. Put the meat into a bowl set over a larger bowl containing iced water. Stir in the carrot, garlic and parsley.

Pour about a third of the duck fat through a fine sieve into a saucepan and heat it up (chill and keep the rest for later use; it makes amazing roast potatoes). Stir about three-quarters of the warm duck fat into the meat with a fork; the mixture should emulsify. Transfer the rabbit mix to a dish and cover with the remaining warm duck fat. Leave in the fridge to set.

Remove the potted rabbit from the fridge 20 minutes before serving so it reaches room temperature. Serve with hot toasted sourdough and cornichons.

Calf's Liver with Bacon and Bubble and Squeak

This delicate dish of grilled calf's liver is the other end of the spectrum from the more visceral, earthy charms of udder and tripe. But liver was always on the Fortnum's menu, as even during the leanest war years offal was unrationed. Calf's liver is key, and as fresh as you can find it. There's nothing like the memory of bad school dinners to really put one off one's lunch.

Bubble and squeak is great, but buttery mash is equally happy alongside.

Serves 4

8 thin slices of calf's liver
2 tablespoons olive oil
8 smoked streaky bacon rashers
salt and freshly ground black pepper

For the sauce
40g unsalted butter
1 shallot, finely chopped
50ml red wine vinegar
20g light soft brown sugar
100ml red wine
250ml beef stock

For the bubble and squeak
550g floury potatoes, such as Maris Piper or red King Edward, peeled and cut into chunks
70g carrot, cut into small dice
140g swede, cut into small dice
100g cabbage, finely shredded
2 teaspoons Worcestershire sauce
2 tablespoons plain flour
40g unsalted butter
2 tablespoons olive oil

First prepare the bubble and squeak. Cook the potatoes in boiling salted water until tender, then drain. In separate pans, cook the carrot, swede and cabbage until tender, then drain thoroughly. Spread them out on a tea towel to dry. Put the potatoes into a bowl and break them up by hand, without mashing them. Season with salt, pepper and the Worcestershire sauce, then mix in the vegetables. Divide the mixture into 4 balls and flatten them so that they are about 4cm thick. Dust them lightly with the flour. Heat the butter and olive oil in a large frying pan. Add the bubble and squeak cakes and fry slowly until crisp and golden on both sides. Keep warm.

Next make the sauce. Melt the butter in a saucepan, add the shallot and cook gently until softened but not coloured. Add the red wine vinegar and the sugar and cook until the liquid has almost completely evaporated. Add the wine and the beef stock and simmer until slightly reduced. Taste and season with salt and pepper if necessary. Keep warm.

Pat the liver slices dry and season with salt and pepper. Heat the olive oil in a large, heavy-based frying pan, then add the liver and cook for 1–2 minutes on each side, until well coloured on the outside but still pink inside. Remove from the pan and keep warm. Add the bacon rashers to the pan and fry until crisp.

To serve, place a bubble and squeak cake in the middle of each serving plate and top with the liver, then the bacon. Pour the sauce around.

Dressed Crab with Marie Rose Sauce

Hard work, sure, extracting every last morsel of native brown crab from its shell. But well worth the hassle. And don't forget the brown meat, the dark, soft part where all that deep-sea flavour lies. If you really can't be bothered to pick your own crab, you can buy it ready-prepared. Put the meat into a ring, with lines of grated or finely chopped egg white alongside grated yolk, and make your Marie Rose sauce. It looks fiddly, but really isn't. Plus you'll end up with excess sauce, always a welcome late-night sight in the fridge.

Serves 4

80g fresh brown crab meat
a squeeze of lemon juice
a pinch of salt
2 eggs
440g fresh white crab meat
2 tablespoons very finely chopped parsley

For the Marie Rose sauce
3½ tablespoons good-quality mayonnaise
1 tablespoon tomato ketchup
½ teaspoon lemon juice
¼ teaspoon Worcestershire sauce
a shake of Tabasco sauce
¼ teaspoon brandy

Check the brown meat over and discard any cartilage. Put it into a blender with the lemon juice and salt. Blend for 30 seconds, then transfer to a bowl, cover and chill for 2 hours. It should set like a very soft mousse.

Put all the ingredients for the Marie Rose sauce into a bowl and mix well. Taste and adjust the seasoning with a little more lemon, Worcestershire sauce or Tabasco, if necessary.

Put the eggs into a saucepan of boiling water and boil for 10 minutes. Drain and refresh in cold water until completely cold – this helps prevent a black ring forming around the yolk.

Carefully pick over the white crab meat for any fragments of shell. Place a 10cm metal ring in the centre of a serving plate and cover the bottom with a layer of the brown crab mousse. Then gently spoon a quarter of the white crab meat on top in an even layer about 1cm deep. Remove the ring. Repeat on 3 more plates with the remaining crab meat. Put a straight line of Marie Rose sauce down the centre of the crab meat – this is easily done using a plastic squeezy bottle, if you have one. Cover the sauce with the chopped parsley.

Shell the eggs and separate the whites from the yolks. Grate each on the fine side of the grater, keeping them separate. Put a neat line of egg yolk on one side of the parsley and a neat line of egg white on the other.

Serve with toast – sourdough is particularly good.

Potted Shrimps

The brown shrimp is in fact a small prawn, and traditionally fished off Lancashire's Morecambe Bay, in the shallows of the outgoing tide. The flavour is intense and naturally sweet, up there with the very best of crustacean meat, and is spiced with a little mace, nutmeg, and a touch of pepper, black and cayenne. Warm, until the butter is melted, then eat with hot toast.

Serves 2

120g unsalted butter
a pinch of ground mace
a pinch of cayenne pepper
a little freshly grated nutmeg
a strip of lemon zest
200g peeled cooked brown shrimps
a drop of Worcestershire sauce
a squeeze of lemon juice
salt and freshly ground white pepper

To serve
grated zest of 1 lime
wholemeal toast
lemon wedges

First clarify the butter: melt it in a small saucepan over a low heat, then carefully pour the clear butter into another saucepan, leaving the milky solids behind. Pour 2–3 tablespoons of the clarified butter into a small jug and set aside.

Add the mace, cayenne, nutmeg and lemon zest to the clarified butter in the pan and simmer very gently for 2 minutes. Remove the lemon zest and stir in 40g of the shrimps with the Worcestershire sauce and lemon juice. Remove from the heat and blend this mixture in a food processor (if it is too small for your food processor, a hand blender will do the job).

Return the mixture to the pan, add the rest of the shrimps and stir over a low heat for 2 minutes without letting it boil. Season with a little salt and white pepper, then remove from the heat.

Divide the shrimps and their butter between 2 ramekins, pressing down to level out the top. If necessary, warm the reserved jug of butter briefly in a microwave so it is liquid again. Pour it over the shrimps so that it covers them in a thin layer and place in the fridge to set.

Bring the potted shrimps to room temperature about 20 minutes before you plan to eat them. Sprinkle with the lime zest and serve with hot wholemeal toast and lemon wedges.

Game Pie

Game, furred and feathered. One of the beauties of seasonal British eating, a delicacy unrivalled anywhere across the globe. The fevered anticipation of that first grouse, shot on 12 August and sped down to Fortnum's, by horse, or train or car, ready for the punters. Then roasted, swift and fierce, and served with thin game juice, a bunch of watercress and game chips (home-made posh crisps). True game greatness.

Or venison, roe, red or muntjac, shot on estates the country over, hung to improve that deep savour, then butchered into fillets, haunches and whole great shoulders. Partridge, woodcock, snipe, teal, widgeon and the rest. Hare, with its rich, idiosyncratic heft, and wild rabbits, skinned and baby pink.

This pie is mighty, but surprisingly subtle, and a fitting end for all that wonderful game.

Serves 6–8

400g venison haunch
200g pheasant breasts
200g grouse (or partridge) breasts
200g pork cheek
100g streaky bacon
6 tablespoons olive oil
2 red onions, diced
2 carrots, diced
2 garlic cloves, crushed
2 tablespoons thyme leaves
125g chestnut mushrooms, cut into halves or quarters
2 tablespoons plain flour
100ml red wine
100ml port
1 bay leaf
400ml beef stock
salt and freshly ground black pepper

Cut all the meat into 5cm dice. Heat half the oil in a large casserole over a medium heat and fry the meat in batches until it is browned all over, seasoning it with salt and pepper as it cooks. Transfer each batch to a plate as it is done.

Heat the remaining oil in the pan, add the onions and carrots and cook gently for about 10 minutes, until softened. Stir in the garlic and thyme, then add the mushrooms and cook for 5 minutes longer. Stir in the flour and cook for 2 minutes. Add the wine, raise the heat and simmer until reduced by half. Repeat with the port. Return the meat to the pan, add the bay leaf, then pour in the stock and bring to a simmer. Cover and transfer to an oven heated to 150°C/Gas Mark 2. Cook for about 1½ hours, until the meat is tender, then remove from the oven and leave to cool. Transfer the mixture to a pie dish.

For the shortcrust pastry
250g plain flour
a pinch of salt
125g unsalted butter
about 3 tablespoons water
1 egg, lightly beaten, to glaze

To make the pastry, sift the flour and salt into a bowl and rub in the butter with your fingertips until the mixture resembles fine breadcrumbs. Stir in enough water to bring it together into a dough, wrap in cling film and leave to rest in the fridge for 30 minutes.

Roll out the pastry to about 4mm thick, ensuring it is large enough to cover the pie dish with some to spare. Cut a long strip to cover the rim of the dish, then moisten the rim with a little water and press the pastry strip on to it. Brush the pastry strip with water. Lift up the rest of the pastry on the rolling pin and use to cover the dish. Trim the edges and then crimp them to seal.

Brush all over with the beaten egg and make a hole in the centre to let out steam. Place in the oven at 180°C/Gas Mark 4 and bake for 30 minutes, until the pastry is golden brown.

Smoked Salmon and Buckwheat Pancake Gâteau

Inspired by a Nico Ladenis classic, this layers buckwheat pancakes with smoked salmon, cream cheese and chives. Cut like a gâteau, in fat slices, and lavish with a tomato and oregano vinaigrette.

Serves 10–12

300g spinach
500g full-fat cream cheese
80ml whipping cream
2 teaspoons lemon juice
grated zest of 1 lemon
a bunch of chives, finely chopped
500g smoked salmon
salt and freshly ground white pepper
sprigs of watercress, to garnish

For the buckwheat pancakes
50g plain flour
100g buckwheat flour
a pinch of salt
2 large eggs
200ml milk
melted unsalted butter, for greasing the pan

For the tomato and oregano vinaigrette
1 shallot, finely sliced
100g ripe tomatoes, diced
200ml tomato passata
1 garlic clove, crushed
1 tablespoon chopped oregano
85ml sherry vinegar
100ml extra virgin olive oil

First make the pancakes. Mix the dry ingredients together in a large bowl and make a well in the centre. Whisk the eggs and milk together, then pour them into the well and gradually mix in the flour from the sides, until you have a smooth batter.

Lightly brush a 20cm non-stick frying pan with melted butter and leave over a moderate heat until hot but not smoking. Pour in a ladleful of the batter, tilting the pan so it covers the base. Cook over a medium heat for 1–2 minutes, until the surface is covered in bubbles and the pancake is golden underneath. Flip and cook for 1 minute more. Transfer to a tray and repeat with the remaining batter, brushing the frying pan with more butter between each pancake. You will need 4 pancakes for the gâteau. It is important that they are about 3 times thicker than normal pancakes so they stabilise the gâteau.

Add the spinach to a large pan of boiling salted water and blanch for 1 minute. Drain well and squeeze out the excess water, then chop finely.

Put three-quarters of the cream cheese in a bowl and mash until smooth (a rubber spatula is good for this), working in some salt and pepper at the same time. Gradually add two-thirds of the whipping cream, stirring and beating until the mixture has a smooth, soft consistency. Now work in the spinach, lemon juice and zest. If the mixture is slightly too firm (it should be spreadable), work in the remaining cream. Finally mix in a quarter of the chopped chives and check the seasoning.

Line the base of a 20cm springform cake tin with baking parchment. Cover the base with one of the pancakes. Cut the smoked salmon into pieces 8–10cm long and make a neat layer of slices on the pancake: start at the outside and push the slices right to the edge, then fill in the centre with straight pieces of salmon. Add a layer of the cream cheese mixture, then alternate these layers – pancake, smoked salmon and cream cheese – finishing with a pancake. Chill for about 4 hours, until set.

Beat the remaining cream cheese until smooth and spreadable. Remove the springform ring from the cake tin and evenly spread the cream cheese in a thin layer over the top and sides. Sprinkle the remaining chopped chives all over, gently pressing them on to the side of the gâteau with your hand.

To make the tomato vinaigrette, put all the ingredients in a bowl and leave to marinate for a few hours. Blend with a handheld electric blender until smooth, then strain through a sieve. Check the seasoning.

The gâteau is best cut into wedges when set firm, then left to reach room temperature for 10–15 minutes before serving – it will soften slightly and the flavour will be better than if you eat it straight from the fridge. Serve the gâteau garnished with watercress sprigs and accompanied by the tomato and oregano vinaigrette.

Overnight-Shoulder-of-Lamb Shepherd's Pie

Shoulder, slow-braised on the bone, for serious depth and heft. With mash, piped (or simply spread) on top. A winter classic, made better still. Pick the meat while still warm, as it makes the job easier. And baking the potatoes first will give you a drier, fluffier mash than the boiled equivalent.

Serves 8

1 shoulder of lamb on the bone
2 carrots, cut into 1cm dice
1 celery stalk, cut into 1cm dice
1 large onion, cut into 1cm dice
8 garlic cloves, finely chopped
a sprig of rosemary, leaves finely chopped
leaves from 4 sprigs of thyme
2–3 tablespoons Worcestershire sauce, to taste
3 tablespoons tomato ketchup
500ml chicken stock
a handful of frozen peas
salt and freshly ground black pepper

For the duchesse potato topping
6 large baking potatoes (about 2kg)
200ml double cream
120g unsalted butter
6 egg yolks

Season the lamb shoulder well and put it on a wire rack in a roasting tray. Cover the tray loosely with foil, place in the oven at 120°C/Gas Mark ½ and slow-roast for about 8 hours – at Fortnum's they normally put it in at the end of a shift so it is ready the next morning. Pick the meat out, removing all fat and skin – it is a lot easier to do this while it is still warm. Shred it into decent-sized pieces.

Heat a spoonful of lamb fat from the roasting tray in a large pan, add the carrots, celery and onion and cook gently until soft. Stir in the garlic and herbs and cook for a couple of minutes longer. Add the Worcestershire sauce, tomato ketchup and the lamb and mix well. Pour in the stock and simmer for 15–20 minutes, until it has reduced but the mixture is still moist. Check the seasoning.

To make the topping, wrap the potatoes in foil and bake at 200°C/Gas Mark 6 for about an hour, until tender. Leave until cool enough to handle, then cut them in half, scoop out the flesh and push it through a potato ricer or a sieve into a bowl. Bring the double cream and butter to the boil in a pan and beat them into the potato. Season well, then mix in the egg yolks. Put the mixture into a piping bag fitted with a star nozzle.

Put the lamb mixture into a large pie dish, pressing it right down. Scatter the frozen peas over, then pipe the duchesse mix on top, covering the filling completely. Place in an oven heated to 180°C/Gas Mark 4 for about 20 minutes, until piping hot and golden brown.

Steak and Kidney Pudding

A Great British dish, hefty but warming, stout and soothing. Like Sultana Bran, the key is in the ratio, ideally three parts beef to one part kidney. Okay, so it's not the lightest of dishes. But that's exactly the point.

Serves 6–8

4 tablespoons olive oil
1 large onion, chopped
150g button mushrooms
1kg chuck steak, cut into 2.5cm cubes
1 tablespoon Worcestershire sauce
½ teaspoon freshly grated nutmeg
25g plain flour
650ml beef stock
300g kidneys, cut into small chunks, white cores removed
salt and freshly ground black pepper

For the suet pastry
375g self-raising flour
1½ teaspoons baking powder
½ teaspoon salt
180g shredded suet
about 220ml iced water

Heat half the oil in a large casserole, add the onion and fry until soft. Add the mushrooms and fry until lightly coloured. Meanwhile, heat the remaining oil in a large, heavy-based frying pan. Season the beef, add to the frying pan and fry in batches over a high heat until sealed all over.

Transfer the meat to the casserole and stir in the Worcestershire sauce, nutmeg and some salt and pepper. Add the flour and cook, stirring, for a couple of minutes. Stir in the stock, bring to a simmer and transfer to an oven heated to 150°C/Gas Mark 2. Cook for 1½–2 hours, until the meat is just tender.

Blanch the kidney pieces in a pan of simmering salted water for 3 minutes, then drain in a sieve. Leave in the sieve for the juices to drain off. Add to the casserole about 15 minutes before the end of cooking. Remove the casserole from the oven and leave to cool.

To make the suet pastry, mix the flour, baking powder and salt together, then stir in the suet. Add enough iced water to bring everything together into a soft dough. Turn out on to a lightly floured board and cut off a quarter to form the pudding lid. Roll out the rest to 4–5mm thick. Use to line the base and sides of a greased 1.5-litre pudding basin and add the filling. Roll out the reserved piece of pastry into a circle. Brush the edges of the pastry lining the basin with water and place the lid on top, pressing the edges together to seal well. Trim off any excess.

Cover with a piece of baking parchment pleated in the centre to allow the pudding to rise. Repeat with pleated foil, then tie string under the rim of the basin to secure. Put in a metal steamer over a pan of simmering water and steam for 2 hours, topping up as necessary with more hot water. (If you don't have a steamer, put the pudding on an upturned saucer in a large saucepan, adding enough hot water to the pan to come two-thirds of the way up the sides of the bowl.)

When the pudding is done, remove the foil and parchment, run a knife around the edge of the bowl and turn out on to a large plate.

Picnics

The picnic certainly wasn't designed with the British climate in mind. Rather than lolling under shady bowers, or feasting under brilliant blue skies, we swap al fresco bliss for a limp sandwich and a lukewarm cup of tea, eaten in the car, accompanied by the pitter-patter of rain falling upon a metal roof. Hardly the Arcadian idyll. More John Betjeman's 'sand in the sandwiches, wasps in the tea'. But the Fortnum's hamper, a fixture since the late eighteenth century, contains enough edible excitement to blast away any unseasonal gloom.

Charles Dickens was a fan. 'Heavens, all the hampers fly wide open and the green downs burst into a blossom of lobster salad!' he wrote of the Fortnum's Derby Day picnic hampers in the mid-nineteenth century. Back in those days, the Fortnum's hamper was as much a part of 'The Season' as breathless Debs and a surfeit of Champagne. And you'd find them everywhere from Ascot and Henley to Goodwood and Cowes. You still do. They could be belly-bustingly lavish too, containing turtle soup, game pie, caviar, foie gras, fruit salad in Cognac and fresh strawberries and cream.

These days, you can still fill your Fortnum's hamper with whatever you dream of and desire. A cold rare fillet of beef, dressed crabs and lobsters, olives, great British hams, potted shrimps and all manner of cold puddings. And now, Fortnum's has created the Hamperling, the hamper's younger brother, small and perfectly formed. Available from Heathrow T5, it's filled with anything from Glenarm beef to smoked salmon and caviar. Exactly what you need to while away that long-haul ennui.

Dickens's lobster salad is a fine, if expensive, picnic dish, as it travels well and requires little more than a fork with which to devour it. And that is at the crux of picnic food – flavour-packed but practical, and elegant without ever being too stuck-up. Simplicity is at its core. There's no place for half-witted tasting menus, or food that's a fiddle to eat.

Pan bagnat, made the previous day, so all that oil and juice soaks into the loaf; fresh dressed crab; a handful of fiery radishes, their green tops still attached, served with cold butter and salt. Home-made taramasalata with pitta; a really good Vichyssoise or gazpacho, slurped from the glass; whole roast chicken, carved with a penknife and eaten with fat blobs of home-made mayonnaise and a really good baguette; a huge game pie, filled with grouse and partridge and hare, enclosed in a beautifully burnished raised crust. Scotch eggs, too, work wonders at picnics, with a smear of English mustard. And sausage rolls and sausages, cold and plump. Even a whole poached salmon or sea trout. Not forgetting fresh strawberries and raspberries with cream, cold treacle tart, Victoria sponge, Bakewell tart, marmalade tea bread and scones. Fortnum's is constantly putting together picnic hampers (filled with everything from Shropshire black ham with celeriac remoulade to lemon posset) for any number, from two to 2,000. You might not be able to rely on the weather. But a handsome, well-thought-out hamper will never let you down.

Savoury Tarts

Made with savoury short pastry, with everything sitting pretty in light, wobbling egg custard. Do not fear the length of the recipes. They may look daunting, but sometimes a little hard work pays big dividends.

Wild Mushroom and Tarragon Tarts

Makes 4

20g unsalted butter
1 small shallot, finely diced
180g wild mushrooms (or oyster mushrooms), sliced
1 tablespoon chopped tarragon
1 egg
130ml double cream
30g Parmesan cheese, grated
salt and freshly ground black pepper

For the savoury pastry
450g plain flour
1 teaspoon salt
2 teaspoons sugar
300g chilled unsalted butter, diced
1 medium egg
20ml milk

First make the pastry. Put the flour, salt and sugar into a food processor, add the butter and whiz until the mixture resembles crumbs. Lightly whisk the egg with the milk, then add to the food processor and pulse to a dough. Turn out, wrap in cling film and chill for at least 30 minutes. (This makes twice as much pastry as you need but the excess will keep in the fridge for 3 days or can be frozen.)

On a lightly floured surface, roll out half the pastry to about 3mm thick and use to line four 10cm tartlet tins. Chill for 30 minutes. Line with baking parchment, fill with baking beans or rice and bake blind for 12 minutes in an oven heated to 180°C/Gas Mark 4. Remove the baking parchment and beans or rice, return the tart cases to the oven and bake for another 3–4 minutes, until the pastry is very lightly coloured.

Melt the butter in a small pan, add the shallot and sweat until soft. Add the mushrooms and a pinch of salt and cook gently until tender, then stir in the tarragon.

Whisk the egg with the double cream and season with salt and pepper. Fill the tart cases with the mushroom mixture, sprinkle over the Parmesan cheese and top up with the egg and cream. Return the tarts to the oven and bake for 12–15 minutes, until the filling is set and the top is lightly coloured.

Stilton and Leek Tarts

Makes 4

½ quantity of Savoury Pastry (see opposite)
30g unsalted butter
2 small leeks, thinly sliced
1 tablespoon thyme leaves
1 egg
130ml double cream
60g Stilton cheese, preferably Cropwell Bishop, crumbled
salt and freshly ground black pepper

On a lightly floured surface, roll out the pastry to about 3mm thick and use to line four 10cm tartlet tins. Chill for 30 minutes. Line with baking parchment, fill with baking beans or rice and bake blind for 12 minutes in an oven heated to 180°C/Gas Mark 4. Remove the baking parchment and beans or rice, return the tart cases to the oven and bake for another 3–4 minutes, until the pastry is very lightly coloured.

Melt the butter in a pan, add the leeks and thyme and season with salt and pepper. Cook until soft but not coloured.

Whisk the egg with the double cream and season with salt and pepper. Put the leeks into the tart cases, scatter over the crumbled Stilton, then top up with the egg and cream. Return the tarts to the oven and bake for 12–15 minutes, until the filling is set and the top is lightly coloured.

Asparagus and Broad Bean Tarts

Makes 4

½ quantity of Savoury Pastry
(see page 100)
100g asparagus
100g shelled broad beans
1 egg
130ml double cream
1 tablespoon chopped curly parsley
salt and freshly ground black pepper

On a lightly floured surface, roll out the pastry to about 3mm thick and use to line four 10cm tartlet tins. Chill for 30 minutes. Line with baking parchment, fill with baking beans or rice and bake blind for 12 minutes in an oven heated to 180°C/Gas Mark 4. Remove the baking parchment and beans or rice, return the tart cases to the oven and bake for another 3–4 minutes, until the pastry is very lightly coloured.

Trim the asparagus and blanch it in boiling salted water for about 2 minutes, until just tender. Drain and refresh in cold water, then cut into 2–3cm lengths. Blanch the broad beans in the same way, then drain and refresh. Slip the beans out of their thin skins.

Whisk the egg with the double cream and season with salt and pepper. Put the asparagus and beans into the tart cases, scatter over the parsley and top up with the egg and double cream. Return the tarts to the oven and bake for 12–15 minutes, until the filling is set and the top is lightly coloured.

Portland Crab and Chive Tarts

Makes 4

½ quantity of Savoury Pastry
(see page 100)
1 egg
130ml double cream
125g fresh white crab meat
60g fresh brown crab meat
1 tablespoon chopped chives
salt and freshly ground black pepper

On a lightly floured surface, roll out the pastry to about 3mm thick and use to line four 10cm tartlet tins. Chill for 30 minutes. Line with baking parchment, fill with baking beans or rice and bake blind for 12 minutes in an oven heated to 180°C/Gas Mark 4. Remove the baking parchment and beans or rice, return the tart cases to the oven and bake for another 3–4 minutes, until the pastry is very lightly coloured.

Whisk the egg with the double cream and season with salt and pepper. Fill the tart cases with the white and brown crab meat, scatter over the chives, then top up with the egg and cream. Return the tarts to the oven and bake for 12–15 minutes, until the filling is set and the top is lightly coloured.

Jackfruit Salad

A whisper of Siam, in the heart of 45 Jermyn St. Jackfruit has a meaty texture, and promises all manner of 'super' benefits. Lift the amount of chilli, if needed, and of lime juice too.

If you can't find jackfruit, green mango will do. Green mango is unripe mango, which is frequently used in Thai food, especially salads. You can find it for sale in Asian shops, as well as online.

Serves 2

60g bean sprouts
200g tinned jackfruit, drained and sliced
2 small carrots, sliced into thin ribbons
¼ cucumber, very thinly sliced
½ bunch of spring onions, sliced thinly on the diagonal
80g daikon radish, very thinly sliced
1 red chilli, deseeded and thinly sliced
2 tablespoons chopped mint
2 tablespoons coriander leaves

For the dressing
50ml rice vinegar
30ml water
25ml lime juice
15g caster sugar
1 red chilli, deseeded and finely diced
1 garlic clove, crushed
¼ teaspoon salt

Put all the ingredients for the dressing in a pan and slowly bring to the boil, stirring to dissolve the sugar. Remove from the heat and leave to cool.

Blanch the bean sprouts in a pan of boiling water for 30 seconds, then drain, refresh in cold water and drain again. Put them into a bowl and add the remaining vegetables, plus the red chilli and herbs. Add the dressing and toss well, then serve straight away.

Fortnum's Waldorf Salad

A Waldorf salad. With pickled walnuts. And no grapes. So not a classic Waldorf salad, but a leaner, meaner version. The original was named after the famed New York hotel, and made more famous still (in the UK, at least), by Basil Fawlty. 'We're out of Waldorfs,' stutters the irascible hotelier, before proceeding to dig his hole ever deeper. The mustard adds much-needed punch.

Serves 4

3 celery sticks, plus a small handful of celery leaves
2 Cox's apples
8 pickled walnuts, sliced

For the mayonnaise
1 large egg yolk
½ teaspoon English mustard
1 teaspoon smooth Dijon mustard
1 teaspoon white wine vinegar
150ml vegetable oil
a squeeze of lemon juice
salt and freshly ground black pepper

First make the mayonnaise. Whisk the egg yolk and mustards in a bowl until thoroughly combined, then whisk in half the white wine vinegar. Add the vegetable oil a few drops at a time, whisking constantly. You can begin to add the oil more quickly once about a third of it has been incorporated and the mayonnaise is stable. Add the rest of the vinegar towards the end. When all the oil has been added, thin the mayonnaise with a little water if it is too thick. Season with lemon juice, salt and pepper to taste.

Peel the celery stalks and slice them thinly on the diagonal. Put them in a bowl. Cut the apples into quarters and remove the core. Slice each quarter thinly and add to the celery. Mix in just enough mayonnaise to coat (you probably won't need it all). Sprinkle the nuts and celery leaves over the top.

Red Salad with Beetroot

Beetroot and various types of radicchio. Feel free to mix and match, to create a winter salad that looks every bit as colourful as it tastes.

This recipe will make more dressing than you need, but it will keep in the fridge for a couple of weeks and can be used for most salads.

Serves 4

- 400g small ruby beetroot
- 600g mixed radicchio, such as Treviso, Chioggia and Tardivo
- 2 teaspoons balsamic vinegar, plus extra to serve
- a few sprigs of red amaranth cress

For the mimosa dressing

- a sprig of tarragon
- 30ml cider vinegar
- juice of ¼ lemon
- 100ml rapeseed oil
- 25ml vegetable oil
- salt and freshly ground black pepper

Whisk all the ingredients for the dressing together in a bowl, or put them in a jar and shake them. Leave overnight for the flavours to infuse if possible.

Put the beetroot on a baking tray, cover with foil and place in an oven heated to 180°C/Gas Mark 4. Bake for 45–60 minutes, until tender. Remove from the oven and leave to cool, still covered. Peel off the skin and cut the beetroot into small wedges.

Separate the radicchio leaves. Put them in a bowl and toss with 50ml of the mimosa dressing and the balsamic vinegar. Toss the beetroot wedges with a little of the dressing to coat them lightly.

Arrange 6 beetroot wedges in a circle on each serving plate. Build up the radicchio leaves in a stack in the centre of each circle. Drizzle a little balsamic vinegar around each plate and add a few sprigs of red amaranth cress.

Ice Cream

'We have a man who makes the best ices in London – bar none. Sometimes he doubts his own skill, so we send him out to eat other people's ices, and when he comes back his confidence is restored, for he realises that he still reigns supreme'

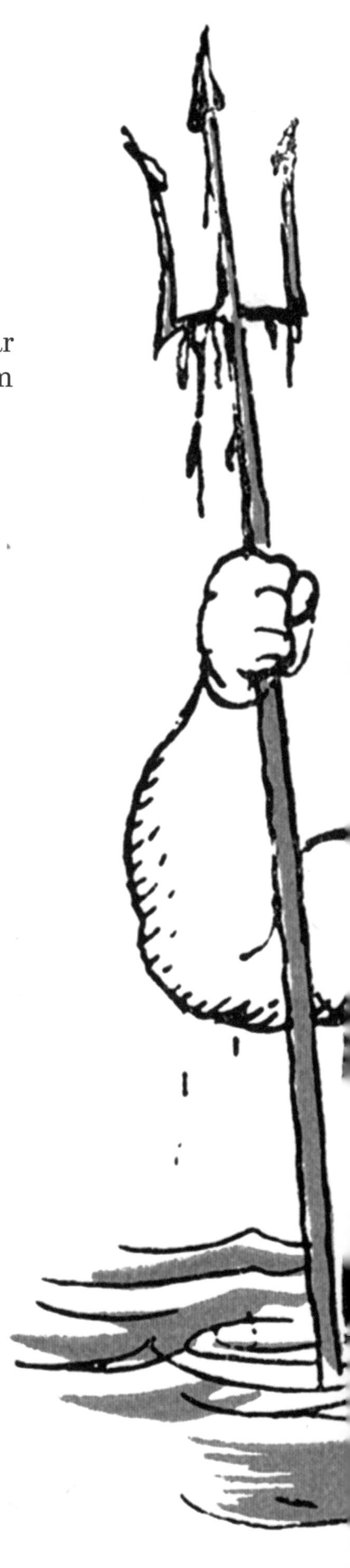

ICES

The Glories of Ice Cream

For generations of greedily excitable children, Fortnum & Mason was about one thing, and one thing only – the legendary Fountain. For it was here, among the linen-topped tables, gleaming Americana and genuine soda fountain, that they could realise their every deep-frozen dream. Vast knickerbocker glories, lavished with fruit, nuts, whipped cream and glacé fruit, plus banana splits, more ice cream and endless sundaes. It opened in 1955, after the last gasp of rationing. During the previous fifteen years, British food had been reduced to its lowest, dullest ebb and children had only had the scantest taste of sugar. Then this, the magical Fountain, a cool, thrilling taste of the USA, a scoop of Uncle Sam in this most British of institutions.

Over 60 years on, The Fountain is no more but Fortnum's ice cream sundaes are still bewitching an entire new generation of children, in The Parlour. Times, tastes and recipes may have changed, but the magic remains the same.

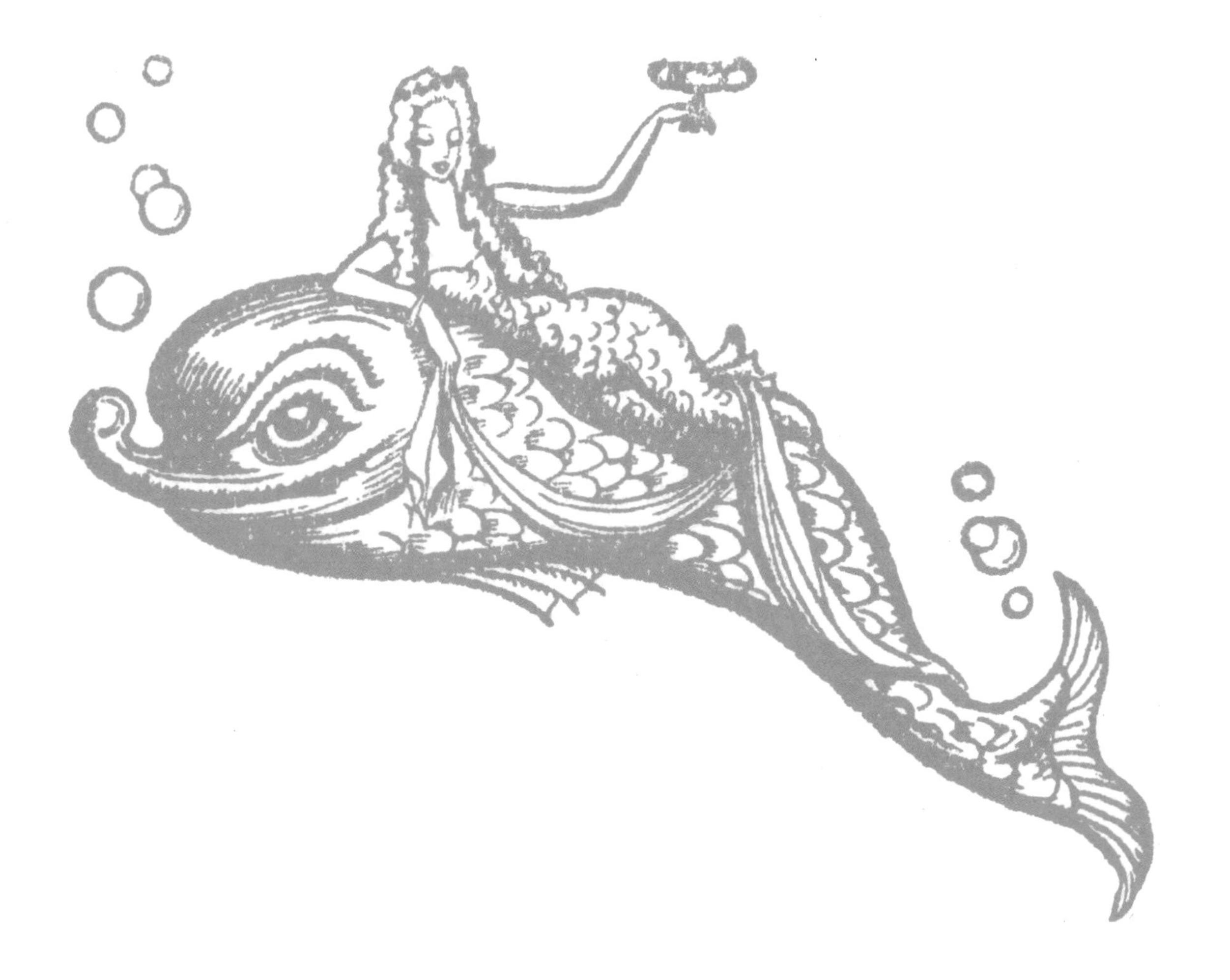

Sundae Basics

Dark Chocolate Sauce

125ml double cream
75ml milk
125g dark chocolate (54 per cent cocoa solids), chopped

Pour the cream and milk into a saucepan and bring to the boil. Remove from the heat, add the chocolate and stir gently until smooth.

Caramel Sauce

150ml double cream
75g dark soft brown sugar
15g unsalted butter

Put the cream and sugar into a small pan and bring to the boil, stirring to dissolve the sugar. Reduce the heat and simmer for 5 minutes. Remove from the heat and stir in the butter until dissolved.

Walnut Sauce

75g walnuts
1 quantity caramel sauce (see above)

Spread the walnuts on a baking sheet and toast in an oven heated to 180°C/Gas Mark 4 for 8–10 minutes, until slightly darker in colour. Stir them into the caramel sauce.

Chantilly Cream

250ml double cream
1 vanilla pod
1 tablespoon icing sugar

Pour the cream into a bowl, then slit the vanilla pod open lengthwise and scrape out the seeds into the bowl. Sift in the icing sugar and whip the cream until it forms soft peaks.

Raspberry Purée

150g fresh or frozen raspberries
icing sugar

Push the raspberries through a sieve to make a purée, discarding the seeds. Sweeten to taste with icing sugar.

Blackcurrant Purée

150g fresh or frozen blackcurrants
40g caster sugar

Put the blackcurrants and sugar into a small pan with a tablespoon of water and cook gently, stirring occasionally, until the blackcurrants are cooked and mushy. Press the mixture through a sieve and leave to cool. Adjust the sweetness to taste, if necessary.

Meringue

As the great Delia Smith once pointed out, the most important ingredient in meringue is not egg whites, but air. All that whisking creates tiny bubbles, essential in creating the perfect meringue: crisp on the outside, while gloriously chewy within. You want to whisk your egg whites and sugar until the mixture stands proudly on its own, in distinctive stiff peaks, like the Alps in soft focus. Do make sure there's not even a whisper of yolk; in this case, fat is not your friend, and will prevent peaky perfection. If you want to use a balloon whisk, go for it. But an electric hand whisk is far easier. And the results exactly the same. Oh, and an Italian meringue is simply meringue made with hot sugar syrup, rather than plain caster sugar. It gives a more voluminous, stiff and reliable end result.

Meringue Sticks and Meringue Buttons

2 medium egg whites
100g caster sugar

Whisk the egg whites until foamy, then whisk in a third of the caster sugar until thick. Add another third of the sugar and whisk until fully incorporated. Add the remaining sugar and whisk until stiff and glossy.

Line a baking sheet with baking parchment. Transfer the meringue to a piping bag fitted with a 5mm star nozzle. For meringue sticks, pipe the meringue onto the baking parchment in straight lines approximately 18cm long. To make meringue buttons, pipe in mounds about 2.5cm in diameter. Place in an oven heated to 80°C (or the lowest possible temperature in a gas oven) and leave until the meringue is completely dry and can be lifted off the baking parchment easily – about 1½ hours for sticks, 2–3 hours for buttons. Leave to cool.

Italian Meringue

2 medium egg whites
100g caster sugar
60ml water

Put the egg whites into a large bowl and set aside. Put the sugar and water into a small, heavy-based pan and heat, stirring, until the sugar has dissolved. Raise the heat and boil, without stirring, until the syrup reaches 118°C on a sugar thermometer.

While the sugar is coming to the boil, whisk the egg whites until they form soft peaks; make sure you keep checking the syrup as you do this, so it doesn't get too hot. When it reaches 118°C, remove it from the heat immediately and pour it onto the egg whites in a slow trickle, whisking constantly. When the syrup has all been incorporated, continue to whisk until the meringue is firm and cool. Bake as required.

Ice Cream Sundaes

Banana Split

A banana. Split. And stuffed full with vanilla, chocolate and strawberry ice cream. Oh, and copious handfuls of nuts, dried fruit and that all-important Maraschino cherry.

Peel a banana and split it lengthwise. Put the banana halves into a long dish and top with a scoop each of vanilla, chocolate and strawberry ice cream. Pipe or spoon some Chantilly cream on top, then add 5 or 6 strawberries, cut into quarters. Drizzle with chocolate sauce and caramel sauce and sprinkle with a few toasted flaked almonds. Decorate with a Maraschino cherry.

Eton Mess Sundae with Lime and Basil

Cut a handful of strawberries into quarters and marinate them with a sprinkling of caster sugar and the juice of 1 lime for 30 minutes or so. Mix in a few shredded basil leaves.

Alternate scoops of vanilla and strawberry ice cream in a tall glass, scattering pieces of broken meringue between them. Spoon the strawberry mixture on top.

Mango and Lime Sundae

Peel, stone and dice a ripe Alphonso mango. Marinate with a sprinkling of caster sugar and the juice of 1 lime for 30 minutes or so. Mix in a few shredded mint leaves. Alternate scoops of mango sorbet and lime sorbet in a tall glass and spoon the mango salsa on top.

Knickerbocker Glory

This garish American concoction (which first appeared on The Fountain menu in 1955) seemed as exotic as Nubian dancing girls to the sugar-starved children of the 50s. My mother and father still talk of the vast ice cream cocktail in hushed, awed tones. 'About the same size as we were,' they whisper, recalling lashings of strawberry and vanilla ice cream, fresh fruit and raspberry syrup and a spoon as long as their arm. These days, Fortnum's add popping candy, Italian meringue and pineapple chunks to make this a sundae to rule them all. A whole generation of children were treated to this before being packed off to boarding school. It almost made the weeks away from home worth it. Almost.

Pour a good tablespoonful of raspberry purée into a tall knickerbocker glory glass and swirl it around to coat the sides. Pipe or spoon in a layer of Chantilly cream, and scatter with a few pieces of diced fresh pineapple and strawberry. Add a scoop of strawberry ice cream, and a scoop of vanilla, then repeat the whole process, sprinkling over a layer of crumbled meringue buttons before adding the final scoop of ice cream. Pipe a generous layer of Italian meringue all over the top and glaze lightly with a blowtorch. Decorate with a meringue stick.

Chocolossus Sundae

This baby's big. With banana and Chocolossus ice cream, walnut sauce, whipped cream, banana chips and Chocolossus biscuits. Forget the Colossus of Rhodes – this sundae truly bestrides the ice cream world.

Swirl some chocolate sauce around the base of a coupe glass. Add a scoop of banana ice cream (see below), then a few dried banana chips, followed by a scoop of chocolate ice cream and a few more dried banana chips. A few mini marshmallows are nice too, as they add another texture. Pipe or spoon some Chantilly cream over the top. Top with 5 chocolate mocha beans, drizzle with chocolate sauce and walnut sauce, then add some more Chantilly cream. At Fortnum's we serve this with two of our supersized, ultra-chocolatey Chocolossus biscuits on the side.

If you can't get any banana ice cream, you can make a very quick and easy one by freezing 4 chopped ripe bananas for at least 2 hours, until completely frozen, then blitzing them in a food processor or blender with 2 tablespoons of honey and the zest and juice of 1 lime. Use immediately.

Dusty Road Sundae

Nothing dry about this much-loved mélange, with coffee and chocolate ice cream draped in caramel sauce, whipped cream, chocolate flakes and decorated with a coffee macaroon.

Swirl some chocolate sauce around the base of a coupe glass. Add a scoop of coffee ice cream, then a scoop of dark chocolate ice cream, followed by another scoop of coffee ice cream and a final scoop of chocolate ice cream. If you can buy some coffee macaroons, break one into quarters and add it between the ice cream layers (if you don't have any macaroons, add some broken meringue buttons). Pipe or spoon a few dollops of Chantilly cream on top. Top with shavings of dark chocolate, drizzle with chocolate sauce and caramel sauce, then place a second macaroon (or meringue) on top, together with two long white chocolate sticks.

Black Velvet Sundae

No, not that heavenly mixture of Guinness and Champagne, rather a study in meringue and blackcurrant. Chunks of meringue, tumbled in with blackcurrants three ways: ice cream, compote, and sauce. Oh, and topped with Chantilly cream.

Make a blackcurrant compote by gently simmering 150g blackcurrants with 50g caster sugar and a cinnamon stick until the currants are soft. Leave to cool, then taste and adjust the sweetness if necessary.

Swirl some blackcurrant sauce around the base of a coupe glass. Add a scoop of vanilla ice cream, then a scoop of blackcurrant ice cream, followed by another scoop of vanilla and a final scoop of blackcurrant, scattering a few broken meringue buttons between each layer. Pipe or spoon some Chantilly cream on top. Drizzle with a little blackcurrant sauce, add a spoonful of the blackcurrant compote, then finish with a white chocolate stick.

This is also very good made with blackcurrant granita instead of ice cream. Make a sugar syrup by heating 150g caster sugar and 150ml water together, stirring until the sugar has dissolved. Bring to the boil and simmer for 1–2 minutes, then remove from the heat. Put it into a food processor or blender with 500g fresh or frozen blackcurrants, 100ml crème de cassis and 1 tablespoon lemon juice and blitz until smooth. Pass through a fine sieve, then freeze in a shallow rectangular container. After about 2 hours, scratch the surface all over with a fork to form ice crystals. Return to the freezer for an hour or so, then repeat until you have a tray full of ice crystals.

Ice Cream Floats For the Young at Heart, But Old of Age

These boozy concoctions have been specially created for 45 Jermyn St., and are a little bit, well, more boozy than the classic children's versions. You can use any brand of alcohol you want, within the confines of the recipe, but the better the quality, the better the float will taste.

Float No. 10

Serves 1

15ml Champagne or sparkling wine (this can be flat, left over from a party)
15g caster sugar
25ml Cocchi Vermouth di Torino
15ml Campari
35ml soda water
2 scoops of orange sorbet, preferably blood orange
a slice of orange (use blood orange, if in season)

Put the Champagne or sparkling wine in a small pan and simmer until reduced by a third. Add the caster sugar and stir until dissolved, then leave to cool. (It's worth making a much larger quantity of this syrup and storing it in the fridge to make other drinks.)

Pour the Vermouth, Campari, Champagne syrup and soda water into a small shaker and shake for 10–15 seconds. Scoop the sorbet into a chilled float glass. Pour the liquid ingredients on top and garnish with the slice of orange.

Float No. 11

Serves 1

45ml blackcurrant and lemon verbena syrup (see below)
35ml gin
50ml soda water
1 scoop of vanilla ice cream
1 scoop of lemon sorbet
a blackcurrant, to garnish

For the blackcurrant and lemon verbena syrup
30g blackcurrants
60g caster sugar
200ml cold-brew lemon verbena tea (made by steeping 20g lemon verbena tea leaves in 200ml cold water for 2 hours, then straining)

To make the blackcurrant and lemon verbena syrup, put all the ingredients in a small pan and bring to the boil. Simmer for 15 minutes, until reduced and thickened, then strain through a fine sieve and leave to cool.

For the float, pour the gin, soda water and 45ml of the syrup (the rest will keep in the fridge for several days) into a measuring jug and stir well. Put the ice cream and sorbet into a chilled float glass, pour over the liquid ingredients and garnish with the blackcurrant.

Afternoon Tea

'Our delightful old recipes are wonderful in sandwiches and other dainties'

Battenberg Cake

Fortnum's has been serving up this multicoloured mélange since 1926. Some say it was created to celebrate the marriage of Princess Victoria (granddaughter to Queen Victoria and mother of Lord Louis Mountbatten) to Prince Louis of Battenberg in 1884. Others claim it was invented in the Prussian village of Battenberg. While yet another group argues it's simply an English cake, named Church Window, which had been around for years before that *arriviste* Battenberg stepped onto our shores. The roots might be murky. But the taste is splendidly straightforward.

During the Great War, though, the Battenberg was an unpatriotic mouthful. The same in World War II, although rationing would have made it difficult to produce. There's even an apocryphal story that it was renamed 'Russian Sponge' from 1939 to 1945.

You can buy a special divided Battenberg tin which allows you to bake four sponges separately; the colours don't bleed together and there is no need to cut the pieces to size.

Beware, this fatless sponge doesn't keep well. Devour as soon as possible. Hardly an onerous task, I know.

Makes a 20cm cake

30g unsalted butter
150g plain flour
5 medium eggs
150g caster sugar
1 vanilla pod
yellow food colouring
red food colouring
⅓–½ jar of apricot jam
icing sugar, for dusting
500g marzipan

Melt the butter over a low heat, then set aside. Sift the flour into a bowl. In a separate bowl, whisk the eggs and sugar with an electric beater until they are pale, thick and greatly increased in volume; the mixture should be thick enough to leave a trail on the surface when the whisk is lifted. In three separate additions, sift the flour over the surface and fold it in with a large metal spoon, being careful to knock as little air out of the mixture as possible. Drizzle the melted butter around the edge of the mixture and fold that in too.

Transfer half the mixture to a separate bowl. Slit the vanilla pod open lengthwise, scrape out the seeds into one of the bowls and fold them in. Then fold a drop of yellow food colouring into the vanilla mixture. Fold a drop of red food colouring into the mixture in the second bowl to give a pale pink colour.

Butter and flour a Battenberg tin and spoon the pink mixture into two of the sections and the yellow mixture into the others. If you don't have a

Battenberg tin, use a small rectangular baking tin, roughly 20cm x 16cm, and position a strip of waxed card lengthwise down the centre to separate the mixtures. Put the pink on one side and the vanilla on the other. Place in an oven heated to 160°C/Gas Mark 3 and bake for 20 minutes, until the sponge is well risen and a skewer inserted into the centre comes out clean. Remove from the oven and leave to cool in the tin.

Run a knife around the edge of the tin and along the dividers. Carefully remove the strips of cake. Trim the tops with a serrated knife, if necessary, so they are flat. If you used an ordinary rectangular tin, cut each piece of cake lengthwise in half and trim as necessary; you need 4 long blocks that are exactly the same size.

Gently heat the apricot jam and strain through a fine sieve. Brush apricot jam along a long side of one pink and one yellow piece of sponge and place them side by side, pressing them gently together so that they stick. Brush the tops with jam. Place the remaining pieces of sponge on top to create a chequerboard pattern, sticking them together with jam as before. If they don't all match up perfectly, trim the sides.

Dust a work surface with a little icing sugar and roll the marzipan out into a rectangle about 4mm thick. The width should be the same as the length of the cake and it should be long enough to wrap right round it. Neaten the edges with a knife and brush the marzipan with the remaining warm jam.

Place the cake at one end of the marzipan, right on the edge. Carefully roll it up, smoothing the marzipan on gently as you go. Trim away any surplus, making sure the join is well sealed. Place with the join underneath and brush off any icing sugar. Trim the short ends of the cake. Lightly score the top with a sharp knife to make a diamond pattern.

Marmalade Tea Bread

Sultanas, soaked in tea, provide the backbone of this classic. And the syrup is also used for a final glaze. The end result is sumptuously soft and moist. It's a particularly good and simple tea bread that you can make with ingredients from the store cupboard as long as you have an orange. Even if you don't, it's hardly a disastrous omission.

Makes 1 large loaf

175g softened unsalted butter
175g light soft brown sugar
grated zest of 1 orange
2 large eggs, lightly beaten
175g self-raising flour
juice of ½ an orange
250g marmalade

Beat the butter, sugar and orange zest together until light and fluffy. Beat in the eggs a little at a time, then sift in the flour and fold it in with a large metal spoon. Fold in the orange juice, followed by 175g of the marmalade.

Transfer the mixture to a greased and lined 900g loaf tin. Place in an oven heated to 160°C/Gas Mark 3 and bake for 45–50 minutes, until the cake is well risen and golden brown and a skewer inserted into the centre comes out clean.

Gently melt the remaining marmalade in a small pan and brush it all over the hot cake. Leave to cool in the tin.

Almond and Raspberry Tarts

Light and lovely. Raspberry jam (or your favourite kind of jam or curd) with frangipane mix on top.

Makes 15

- ½ quantity of Sweet Pastry (see page 242)
- 15 heaped teaspoons raspberry jam
- 120g softened unsalted butter
- 80g caster sugar
- 2 eggs
- 70g ground almonds
- 50g plain flour, plus extra for dusting
- ½ teaspoon baking powder
- 1 teaspoon almond extract
- a little desiccated coconut, for sprinkling
- a little icing sugar, for dusting

Roll out the pastry on a lightly floured surface to 3–4mm thick. Cut out circles with a pastry cutter and use to line 15 bun tins. Put a heaped teaspoon of raspberry jam in each one.

Put the butter and caster sugar into a bowl and cream together until light and fluffy. Beat in one of the eggs, add a spoonful of the ground almonds, then beat in the remaining egg, followed by the remaining ground almonds. Sift in the flour and baking powder and fold them in with a large metal spoon. Finally, fold in the almond extract.

Divide the mixture between the pastry cases, making sure that the jam is completely covered. Sprinkle a light layer of desiccated coconut on top. Place in an oven heated to 160°C/Gas Mark 4 and bake for 20–25 minutes, until golden brown and slightly risen. Remove from the oven and leave to cool. Dust the tarts with icing sugar before serving.

The Art of the Sandwich

I've never entirely bought the official history of the sandwich. You know, the one about the Earl of Sandwich being so deep into his game of cards that he demanded meat be brought to him between two slabs of bread. Just so the lazy sod didn't have to shift his pampered backside from the table. Surely, in a country that venerates both beef and bread, someone might have chanced upon this combination before.

Still, at Fortnum & Mason, the sandwich is no mere belly-stuffer, to be eaten dead-eyed behind your desk. Rather an art all unto itself, and one taken every bit as seriously as any éclair, scone or terrine. Quite rightly too. For those whose tastes veer towards the savoury (like me), it's the highlight of Afternoon Tea in The Diamond Jubilee Tea Salon. On a busy day, the Fortnum's kitchen can churn out over 1,000 rounds of four different varieties of sandwich. That's 4,000 immaculately sliced, identically-sized fingers, soft, pliant and gloriously fresh. I say 'churn', but that's to do the chefs a disservice. Because the sandwich at Fortnum & Mason has its own section of the kitchen, a cool, quiet corner far removed from the usual steam, clatter and hiss.

And it's here, from dawn until dusk, that a chef (two at the weekend) sits, building cucumber on white bread, smoked salmon on brown, egg mayonnaise in poppy seed and Coronation chicken within granary for an endless stream of hungry punters. The process is as strict as it is unbending. Fresh bread, obviously. Fillings mixed fresh every few hours. Not too soggy or wet, as this would stain and sully the bread. And just the right amount of filling, about a quarter to half of the sandwich. Then they lose their crusts, and are sliced into soldiers of exactly the same proportions before being gently pressed, for 30 minutes, beneath a light wooden tray. Nothing is left to chance. If they have to sit around for more than a few minutes (rare, admittedly), they're stored under a damp cloth to preserve their elegantly soft charms.

As to the fillings. The classic cucumber is peeled and cut into thin slices. The cream cheese has a little salt added, before it's spread, gently, over the cut cucumber. Smoked salmon uses just the classic house cure (no cheap, greasy offcuts here), while egg mayonnaise and Coronation chicken are always made fresh. The true art, though, lies in that eternal consistency, making each round look exactly the same. This may sound easy, but it ain't – it takes experience, concentration and a very steady hand. So no workaday plate of sandwiches, rather the obsessive end result of many years' experience. Really, we wouldn't expect anything less.

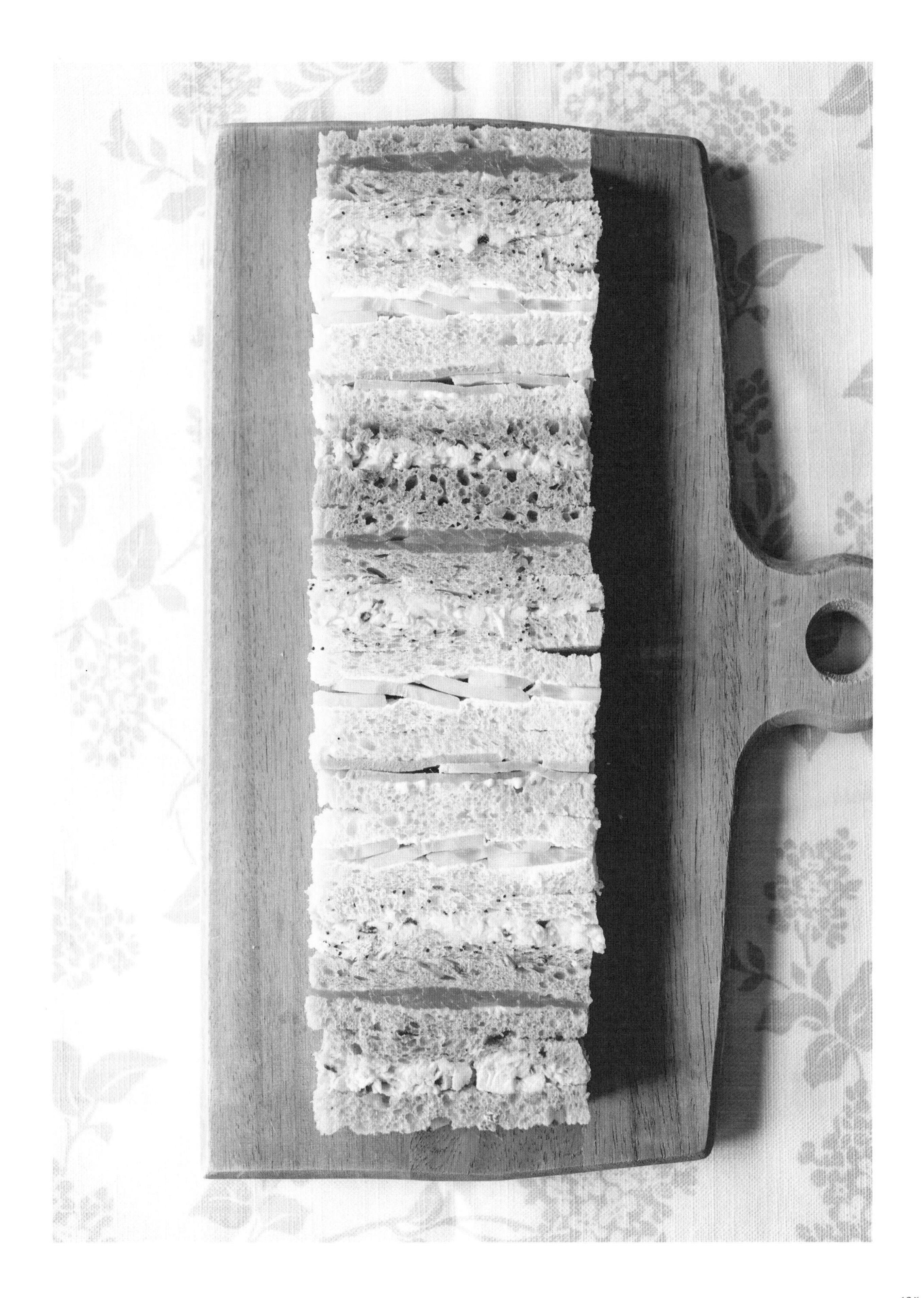

Afternoon Tea Sandwiches

Cucumber with Mint Cream Cheese

A taste of summer all year round, with a gentle sigh of mint and a subtle, citric tang. The salting removes excess water and stops the sandwiches from going soggy. Once made, press lightly with a plate before cutting into fingers.

Makes 16 finger sandwiches

1 cucumber
200g cream cheese
2 tablespoons chopped mint
juice and grated zest of ½ lemon
8 large slices of white bread
butter, for spreading
salt and freshly ground white pepper

Peel the cucumber and trim it so it is the same length as the slices of bread. Slice the cucumber very thinly lengthwise, put the slices on a board and sprinkle lightly with salt. Leave for 20 minutes, then pat dry.

Put the cream cheese into a bowl and beat in the mint, lemon juice and zest and some salt and pepper.

Lightly butter the bread and spread it with the cream cheese mixture. Neatly arrange the cucumber on half the slices of bread, then sandwich together with the remainder. Cut the crusts off and cut each sandwich into 4 fingers.

Coronation Chicken

Created by Rosemary Hume (of Constance Spry fame) in 1953, for Coronation buffets everywhere, this curried chicken concoction had its roots in a similarly high-born creation, Jubilee Chicken, prepared for the Silver Jubilee of George V in 1935.

The Fortnum's version omits the original nuts, uses fresh coriander, plus plump raisins, mango chutney and a little spice to keep all that naughty sweetness in check.

Makes 16 finger sandwiches

1 tablespoon vegetable oil
1½ tablespoons mild curry powder
1 teaspoon turmeric
3 cooked chicken breasts, skinned and finely diced
8–9 tablespoons good-quality mayonnaise
3 tablespoons mango chutney
1 tablespoon chopped golden raisins
2 tablespoons chopped coriander
salt and freshly ground black pepper
butter, for spreading
8 large slices of white bread

Gently heat the vegetable oil in a small pan, add the curry powder and turmeric and cook over a very low heat for 1 minute, stirring constantly. Remove from the heat and cool slightly. Put the diced chicken into a bowl, add the spice mixture and rub it into the chicken. Add the mayonnaise, mango chutney and raisins and mix well. Fold in the chopped coriander and season to taste.

Lightly butter the bread and spread the Coronation chicken mixture over half the slices. Sandwich together with the remaining bread, cut the crusts off, then cut each sandwich into 4 fingers.

Smoked Salmon with Tartare Dressing

The classic smoked salmon sandwich, with extra tartare punch. Don't be mean with the salmon, as it's the star of the show. The Fortnum's house cure is a light smoke, and made from Var salmon, one of the finest and most sustainably farmed salmons you can find. Add a dribble of lemon to the tartare mix if you want a little added bite. Make extra tartare and serve with fish fingers or fish and chips.

Makes 16 finger sandwiches

100g good-quality mayonnaise
15g capers, finely chopped
15g baby gherkins, finely chopped
1 tablespoon chopped dill
1 tablespoon chopped chives
butter, for spreading
8 large slices of granary bread
160g smoked salmon

Mix together the mayonnaise, capers, gherkins, dill and chives.

Lightly butter the bread and spread half the slices with the tartare dressing. Top with the smoked salmon and sandwich together with the remaining bread. Cut the crusts off, then cut each sandwich into 4 fingers.

Egg and Mustard Cress

This reminds me of childhood, when we grew mustard or cress, from seed, on cotton wool. I love the peppery punch, mixed in with the rich mayonnaise. For those with a taste for the piquant, you could add a little Gentleman's Relish to the mix. Or, alternatively, a dash or two of Tabasco. And if poppy seed bread proves difficult to find, then brown or white will do just fine.

Makes 8 finger sandwiches

3 large eggs
75g good-quality mayonnaise
a punnet of mustard and cress
  (or salad cress)
butter, for spreading
8 slices of poppy seed bread
salt and freshly ground black pepper

Boil the eggs for 10 minutes, so the yolks are completely hard. Drain, then cool under cold running water. Peel them and grate on the coarser side of a grater, as you would for cheese. Mix the grated egg with the mayonnaise and cress and season to taste.

Lightly butter the bread and spread the egg mayonnaise over half the slices. Sandwich together with the remaining bread, cut the crusts off, then cut each sandwich into 2 fingers.

Roast Ham with Grain Mustard Dressing

Ham, the real old-fashioned stuff, with a dry texture and deep, piggy tang. Miles removed from those sweaty, soggy re-formed slices of mass-market depression. It might seem quite an operation to cook your gammon to make sandwiches, but the end result is wonderful. I tend to cook a rather bigger piece of gammon, so that I have enough left for lunch with fried eggs and chips.

Makes 16 finger sandwiches

30g English mustard
35g clear honey
20g dark soft brown sugar
2 bay leaves
150ml water
900g piece of unsmoked gammon
butter, for spreading
8 large slices of wholemeal bread

For the grain mustard dressing
80g good-quality mayonnaise
2 teaspoons grain mustard
1 tablespoon chopped tarragon

Put the English mustard, honey, sugar, bay leaves and water into a casserole that is just large enough to hold the gammon. Bring to the boil, stirring to dissolve the sugar, then add the gammon. Turn it over to coat it in the mixture, then cover the casserole and transfer to an oven heated to 140°C/Gas Mark 1. Cook for 1 hour, basting occasionally.

Raise the oven temperature to 190°C/Gas Mark 5, transfer the ham to a small roasting tin and roast for 30 minutes. It will start to colour, so check that it doesn't burn. Remove from the oven and leave to cool.

To make the dressing, mix all the ingredients together in a bowl. Slice the ham thinly. Butter the bread and spread half the slices with the dressing. Cover with the ham, sandwich together with the remaining bread, then cut the crusts off and cut each sandwich into 4 fingers.

Sachertorte

The Fortnum & Mason version of this Austrian chocolate classic is a little different from the norm, in that it contains no apricot jam. Why? Because Garfield Weston, who bought the store in 1951, hated the stuff. And what the boss says, goes.

Makes a 20cm cake

250g plain flour
60g ground almonds
30g cocoa powder
250g dark chocolate (with 55 per cent cocoa solids)
250g softened unsalted butter
310g caster sugar
10 egg yolks
8 egg whites
gold leaf, to decorate (optional)

For the chocolate ganache
200ml double cream
40ml liquid glucose
160g dark chocolate (with 55 per cent cocoa solids), chopped

For the chocolate glaze
10g gelatine leaves
175ml water
135ml double cream
225g caster sugar
75g cocoa powder

Sift the flour, ground almonds and cocoa powder together and set aside. Break up the chocolate and put it in a bowl set over a pan of gently simmering water, making sure the water isn't touching the base of the bowl. Leave until melted. Meanwhile, cream the butter and 250g of the sugar together in a large bowl until light and fluffy. Beat in the egg yolks, 2 at a time, then fold in the melted chocolate, followed by half the sifted flour mixture.

In a separate bowl, whisk the egg whites until they form soft peaks, then gradually add the remaining sugar, whisking until smooth peaks are formed. Stir a large spoonful of the meringue into the chocolate mix to loosen it, then fold in the remaining flour mixture. Fold in the remaining meringue.

Divide between 2 greased and base-lined deep 20cm springform cake tins. Bake in an oven heated to 160°C/Gas Mark 3 for 30–40 minutes, until a skewer inserted in the centre comes out clean. Remove from the oven and leave in the tins for 5–10 minutes before turning out on to a wire rack to cool completely.

To make the chocolate ganache, bring the cream and glucose to the boil. Remove from the heat, add the chocolate and whisk until smooth. Leave until it has thickened to a spreadable consistency, then sandwich the cakes together with it and spread a thin layer over the top and sides.

For the chocolate glaze, soak the gelatine in a bowl of cold water for about 5 minutes, until pliable. Put the water, cream and sugar in a pan and bring to the boil, stirring to dissolve the sugar. Whisk in the cocoa and turn the heat down. Simmer, stirring constantly, for 5–8 minutes, until the mixture is smooth and glossy. Squeeze the excess water out of the gelatine. Remove the glaze from the heat, add the gelatine and stir until dissolved. Leave to cool and thicken. Pour the glaze over the cake, smoothing it on to cover it completely. When the glaze has set, decorate with a little gold leaf, if liked.

Victoria Sandwich Cake

The classic, and perhaps the Queen of English cakes. Which is fitting, as it is named after the Empress of India herself. The key is light sponge, and lashings of the best jam you can find. Like Fortnum's strawberry or raspberry preserve.

Makes a 20cm cake

225g plain flour
15g baking powder
240g softened unsalted butter
240g caster sugar
4 large eggs, at room temperature, lightly beaten
icing sugar, for dusting

For the filling
150g strawberry jam
250ml double cream
250g strawberries, hulled and sliced

Sift the flour and baking powder into a bowl and set aside. In a separate bowl, cream the butter and sugar together until light and fluffy. Beat in the eggs a little at a time, adding a spoonful of the flour if the mixture threatens to separate. Sift in the flour in 3 separate additions, folding it in with a large metal spoon.

Divide the mixture between 2 greased and base-lined 20cm sandwich tins. Place in an oven heated to 180°C/Gas Mark 4 and bake for 25–30 minutes, until the cakes are golden brown and well risen and a skewer inserted in the centre comes out clean. Leave in the tins for 10 minutes, then turn out on to a wire rack to cool completely.

Spread the strawberry jam over one cake and place on a plate. Whip the cream until it forms soft peaks and pipe or spread it over the jam. Cover with the sliced strawberries, place the other cake on top and dust with icing sugar.

Victoria Sandwich Cake with Pastry Cream and Elderflower Jelly

The top of this cake is covered with crème diplomat – pastry cream with whipped cream folded in – plus wonderfully wobbling elderflower-scented jelly cubes. And handfuls of fresh berries too. The recipe may look complicated, but any half-decent baker will make light work of it as it's separated into perfectly easy stages.

Makes a 20cm cake

225g plain flour
15g baking powder
1 vanilla pod
240g softened unsalted butter
240g caster sugar
4 large eggs, at room temperature, lightly beaten
200g mixed summer berries

For the elderflower jelly
8g gelatine leaves
200ml elderflower cordial (undiluted)

For the pastry cream
1 vanilla pod
500ml whole milk
125g caster sugar
6 large egg yolks
40g cornflour
40g unsalted butter

For the crème diplomat
250ml double cream

Sift the flour and baking powder into a bowl and set aside. Slit the vanilla pod open lengthwise and scrape out the seeds with the point of a sharp knife. Put them into a large bowl with the butter and sugar, and cream together until light and fluffy. Beat in the eggs a little at a time, adding a spoonful of the flour if the mixture threatens to separate. Sift in the flour in 3 separate additions, folding it in with a large metal spoon.

Divide the mixture between 2 greased and base-lined 20cm sandwich tins. Place in an oven heated to 180°C/Gas Mark 4 and bake for 25–30 minutes, until the cakes are golden brown and well risen and a skewer inserted into the centre comes out clean. Leave in the tins for 10 minutes, then turn out on to a wire rack to cool completely.

For the elderflower jelly, soak the gelatine leaves in cold water for about 5 minutes. Heat the elderflower cordial in a small pan. Lift the gelatine out of the water, gently squeezing out the excess liquid, and add to the cordial. Stir until completely dissolved. Pour into a small container, such as a plastic tub, and leave to cool, then put it into the fridge to set. Turn the jelly out of the container and cut it into little cubes (you won't need all of it for the cake but it's impractical to make a smaller quantity).

Next make the pastry cream. Slit the vanilla pod open lengthwise and scrape out the seeds. Put the pod and seeds in a pan with the milk and bring to the boil, then remove from the heat and set aside. Beat the sugar, egg yolks and cornflour together in a large bowl. Gradually pour on the hot milk, whisking well. Pass the mixture through a fine sieve back into the pan and cook over a low to medium heat, stirring constantly, until it thickens. It might go lumpy as it starts to thicken but just keep stirring and it will become smooth again. Reduce the heat and cook gently for 2 minutes. Remove from the heat and stir in the butter, then transfer to a bowl. Press a sheet of cling film over the surface and leave to cool.

To make the crème diplomat, put 200g of the pastry cream into a separate bowl. Whisk the double cream until it forms soft peaks, then fold it into the 200g pastry cream.

To assemble, spread one cake with pastry cream and top with the second cake. Spread the crème diplomat over the top and scatter over the summer berries and cubes of elderflower jelly.

Royal Blend Tea Loaf

The loaf is subtly scented, rather than bludgeoned by Fortnum's Royal Blend tea, which is a mixture of Assam tea and Flowery Pekoe from Ceylon. But you can use any good Flowery Pekoe or Assam.

Makes 1 large loaf

350g sultanas
300ml hot water
1½ teaspoons Royal Blend tea leaves
225g light muscovado sugar
275g plain flour
15g baking powder
grated zest of 1 lemon
1 egg, lightly beaten

For the tea syrup
100g caster sugar
100ml water
grated zest of ½ lemon
1 teaspoon Royal Blend tea leaves

For the tea-flavoured apricot glaze (optional)
1 teaspoon Royal Blend tea leaves
75g apricot jam

Put the sultanas into a shallow dish. Pour the hot water over the tea leaves and leave to infuse for 5–10 minutes. Strain the tea and pour it over the sultanas. Leave to soak for at least 2 hours, preferably overnight.

Transfer the sultanas to a mixing bowl, along with any liquid that hasn't been absorbed. Add the sugar, flour, baking powder, lemon zest and egg, and mix well with a wooden spoon. Transfer to a greased and lined 1kg loaf tin. Place in an oven heated to 150°C/Gas Mark 2 and bake for 1–1¼ hours, until the loaf is well risen and a skewer inserted in the centre comes out clean.

While the cake is baking, prepare the tea syrup: combine the sugar, water and lemon zest in a small pan and bring to the boil, stirring to dissolve the sugar. Reduce the heat and simmer for 3–5 seconds. Stir in the tea leaves, cover and leave to stand for 15 minutes.

When the cake is done, remove it from the oven and spike it all over using a cocktail stick. Ensure you reach right to the bottom of the cake, so the syrup can penetrate all the way through. Strain the warm syrup and drizzle it evenly over the cake. Leave in the tin for at least 15 minutes, then turn out on to a wire rack to cool.

If you want to add the apricot glaze, pour 25ml hot water over the tea leaves and leave to infuse for 5 minutes, then strain into a small saucepan. Add the jam and heat gently, stirring until smooth. Strain through a fine sieve into a bowl and brush all over the top of the cake.

Rose Éclairs

As ever, the trick is in the choux pastry. Leave it in the oven a little longer than you expect for best results. Buy a good-quality rosewater; I like the Turkish stuff, which you can easily find on the internet.

Makes 20

For the choux pastry
100g plain flour
75ml whole milk
75ml water
75g unsalted butter, diced
3 medium eggs, lightly beaten

For the rose pastry cream
1 vanilla pod
400ml whole milk
100g caster sugar
8 large egg yolks
30g cornflour
20g unsalted butter
4 teaspoons rosewater, or to taste
120ml double cream

For the fondant icing
300g icing sugar
2 teaspoons lemon juice
about 2 tablespoons water
a little pink food colouring
a few fresh, unsprayed rose petals, to decorate (optional)

First make the choux pastry. Sift the flour on to a small sheet of baking parchment. Put the milk, water and butter into a saucepan over a medium heat. When the butter has melted and the mixture has come to the boil, immediately remove from the heat and beat in the flour with a wooden spoon. Return to the heat and cook, stirring, for 2 minutes. Leave to cool for 5–10 minutes, so it is warm rather than hot. Using a hand-held electric mixer, beat in the eggs a little at a time until they are fully incorporated. The mixture should be thick and glossy and should fall from a spoon if you shake it slightly.

Transfer the choux pastry to a piping bag fitted with a 1cm nozzle. Pipe it on to 2 baking trays lined with baking parchment in thin strips 9–10cm long. Space them at least 5cm apart, as they will expand a lot during baking. Place in an oven heated to 200°C/Gas Mark 6 and bake for 25 minutes, until well risen and golden brown. They should sound crisp and hollow if you tap them underneath. Transfer to a wire rack and leave to cool.

Next make the pastry cream. Slit the vanilla pod open lengthwise and scrape out the seeds. Put the pod and seeds into a pan with the milk and bring to the boil, then remove from the heat and set aside. Beat the sugar, egg yolks and cornflour together in a large bowl. Gradually pour on the hot milk, whisking well. Return the mixture to the pan and cook over a low to medium heat, stirring constantly, until it thickens. It might go lumpy as it starts to thicken, but just keep stirring and it will become smooth again. Reduce the heat and cook gently for 2 minutes. Remove from the heat and mix in the butter, followed by the rosewater, then transfer to a bowl. Press a sheet of cling film over the surface and leave to cool.

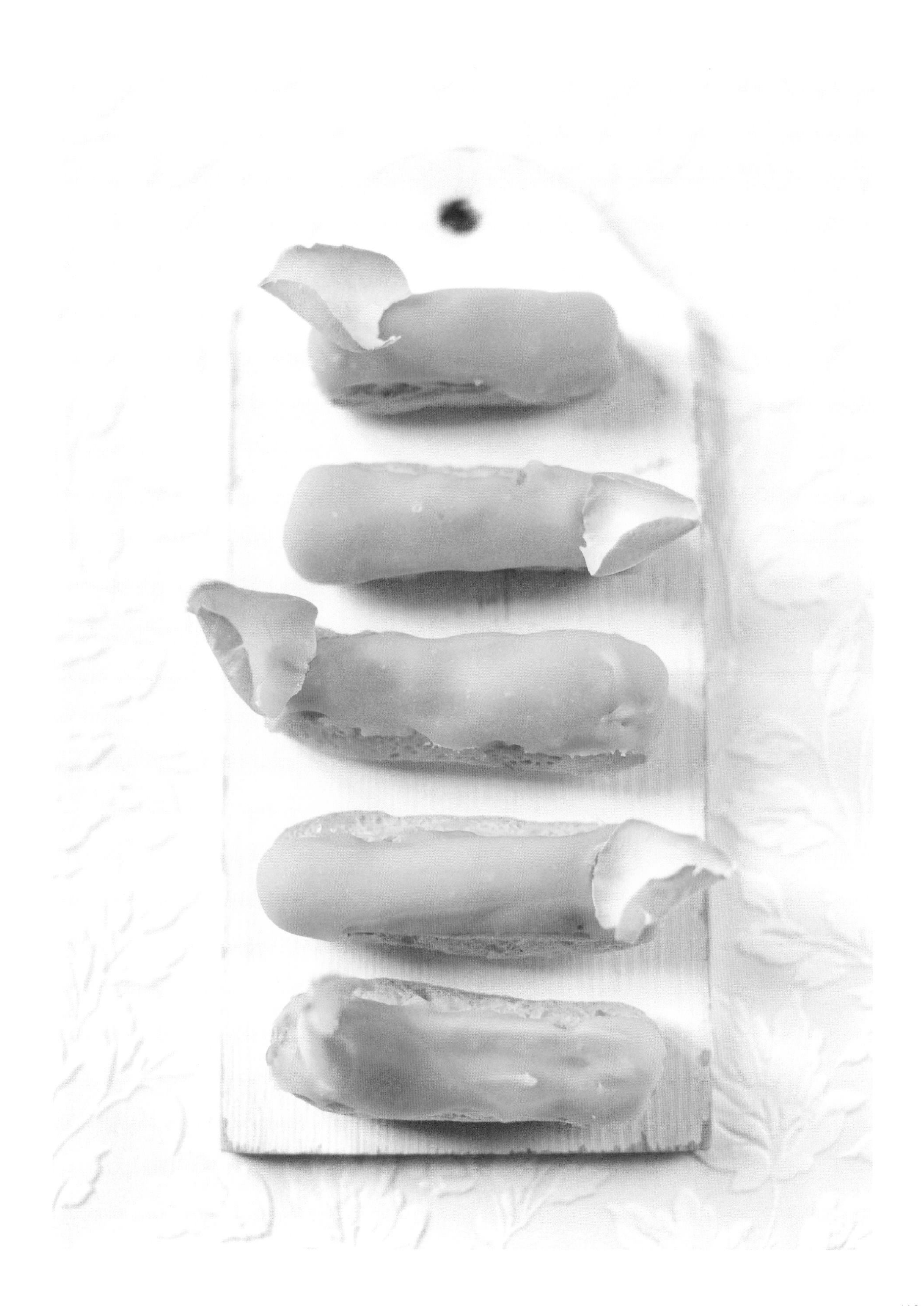

Whip the double cream to soft peaks. Stir the pastry cream vigorously to loosen it a little, then fold in the double cream. Taste and add a little more rosewater, if necessary. Transfer the mixture to a piping bag fitted with a 5mm nozzle. Make a small hole in the tip of each éclair, insert the nozzle, and pipe in the pastry cream until generously filled.

To make the fondant icing, sift the icing sugar into a bowl and stir in the lemon juice. Gradually add enough water to give a mixture the consistency of thick treacle. Stir in the food colouring a drop at a time until you have a pale pink colour. Dip the éclairs in the icing so the tops are generously covered, then leave to set. Once set, decorate with the rose petals, if using.

Scones

Scone. Like gone. Not scone, like stone. The outside should be pale gold, and offer a moment of resistance to the front teeth, before succumbing to their advance, and showing off its soft and warm centre. Slather with clotted cream, and jam. Here endeth the lesson.

These scones are miraculously light (thanks, in part, to the '00' flour, and the double resting period) and are the best I've ever tasted.

Makes about 15

400g '00' flour
20g baking powder
½ teaspoon salt
115g unsalted butter, diced
80g caster sugar
175ml whole milk
1 egg, lightly beaten, to glaze
icing sugar, for dusting

Sift the flour, baking powder and salt into a bowl, then add the butter and rub it in with your fingertips until the mixture resembles fine crumbs. Stir in the sugar, add the milk and mix to give a soft dough; do not over-mix or the scones will be heavy. Cover the bowl with cling film and leave to rest for 30 minutes.

On a lightly floured work surface, roll out the dough to about 1.5cm thick. Cut out rounds with a 5.5cm cutter, re-rolling the trimmings where necessary. Place the scones on a baking sheet lined with baking parchment. Brush with the beaten egg and leave to rest for another 30 minutes.

Place in an oven heated to 180°C/Gas Mark 4 and bake for 12–15 minutes, until well risen and golden brown. Transfer the scones to a wire rack to cool, and dust with icing sugar before serving.

Variation: Sultana Scones
To make sultana scones, follow the recipe above, stirring in 50g sultanas before adding the milk.

Brown Crab Scones

Too often, we ignore the brown crab meat in favour of the more elegant strands of white. But it has a wonderful bosky depth – the red wine, if you will, to the white. This gives these crab scones a wonderful maritime profundity, singing softly of the sea. You can, of course, buy the brown meat separately, but I find picking crabs rather soothing. Save the white for sandwiches, and throw the brown into these scones.

Makes about 10

360g '00' flour
20g baking powder
½ teaspoon salt
105g unsalted butter, diced
25g Parmesan cheese, grated
100g brown crab meat
grated zest of 1 lemon
175ml milk
1 egg, lightly beaten, to glaze

Sift the flour, baking powder and salt into a bowl, then add the butter and rub it in with your fingertips until the mixture resembles fine crumbs. Stir in the Parmesan cheese, brown crab meat and lemon zest. Add the milk and mix until everything comes together into a soft dough; do not over-mix or the scones will be heavy. Cover the bowl with cling film and leave to rest for 30 minutes.

On a lightly floured work surface, roll out the dough to about 1.5cm thick. Cut out rounds with a 5.5cm cutter, re-rolling the trimmings where necessary. Place the scones on a baking sheet lined with baking parchment. Brush with the beaten egg and leave to rest for another 30 minutes.

Place in an oven heated to 180°C/Gas Mark 4 and bake for 12–15 minutes, until well risen and golden brown. Transfer the scones to a wire rack to cool.

Cheddar Cheese and Caramelised Onion Scones

A classic combination of flavours. The onion will take a good thirty minutes to brown, which might seem over the top for scones, but it's definitely worth the wait.

Makes about 10

360g '00' flour
20g baking powder
½ teaspoon salt
105g unsalted butter, diced
25g Parmesan cheese, grated
60g Cheddar cheese, grated
175ml whole milk
1 egg, lightly beaten, to glaze

For the caramelised onion
25g unsalted butter
1 large onion, finely diced
a pinch of salt

For the caramelised onion, melt the butter in a pan, add the onion and salt, then cover and cook gently until soft. Uncover the pan, raise the heat and cook, stirring occasionally, until the onion is lightly browned and very tender. Remove from the heat and set aside.

Sift the flour, baking powder and salt into a bowl, add the butter and rub it in with your fingertips until the mixture resembles fine crumbs. Stir in the cheeses and the caramelised onion. Add the milk and mix until everything comes together into a soft dough; do not over-mix or the scones will be heavy. Cover the bowl with cling film and leave to rest for 30 minutes.

On a lightly floured work surface, roll out the dough to about 1.5cm thick. Cut out rounds with a 5.5cm cutter, re-rolling the trimmings where necessary. Place the scones on a baking sheet lined with baking parchment. Brush with the beaten egg and leave to rest for another 30 minutes.

Place in an oven heated to 180°C/Gas Mark 4 and bake for 12–15 minutes, until well risen and golden brown. Transfer the scones to a wire rack to cool.

Stilton and Blueberry Scones

Fortnum's have been selling Stilton since at least 1849, and have been using the same creamery for the past 40 years. 'Stiltons from Leicestershire farms' cries a Commentary of the 1920s, 'of the sort most favoured by the nobility and the gentry who delve into them with fierce abandon.'

The blueberry jam is quite subtle and simply adds a slight sweetness.

Makes about 10

- 360g '00' flour
- 20g baking powder
- ½ teaspoon salt
- 105g unsalted butter, diced
- 85g Stilton, crumbled
- 20g Parmesan cheese, freshly grated
- 25g blueberry jam
- 120ml whole milk
- 1 egg, lightly beaten, to glaze

Sift the flour, baking powder and salt into a bowl, then add the butter and rub it in with your fingertips until the mixture resembles fine crumbs. Stir in 50g of the Stilton, plus the grated Parmesan and the blueberry jam. Add the milk and mix until everything comes together into a soft dough; do not over-mix or the scones will be heavy. Cover the bowl with cling film and leave to rest for 30 minutes.

On a lightly floured work surface, roll out the dough to about 1.5cm thick. Cut out rounds with a 5.5cm cutter, re-rolling the trimmings where necessary. Place the scones on a baking sheet lined with baking parchment. Brush with the beaten egg, scatter over the rest of the Stilton and leave to rest for another 30 minutes.

Place in an oven heated to 180°C/Gas Mark 4 and bake for 12–15 minutes, until well risen and golden brown. Transfer the scones to a wire rack to cool.

Savouries

'From the deeps of the Seven Seas to the eyries of the mountains, every remoteness is ransacked for quaint and stimulating novelties'

Savouries

Ah, the savoury, that bite-sized hit of piquant power, traditionally served after stolid pudding and before coquettish fruit. In short, the penultimate gasp of a truly civilised dinner. Scotch Woodcock and Welsh Rarebit, Devils and Angels on Horseback and Canapés Ivanhoe . . . who could resist their manifold charms? 'Robustly and triumphantly British,' exclaimed *bon viveur* polemicist P. Morton Shand. Sure, there's always cheese. But the savoury is a course to adore.

Their role was as sop and stimulant. The Special Forces, if you like, of the evening meal, there to exterminate, with extreme prejudice, the last unsatisfied baddies of a trencherman's greed. With all those manly, strident flavours, they were seen very much as a gentleman's relish, far more at home in the wood- and waffle-panelled dining rooms of the old St James's clubs than they were in the more genteel salons of the modern lady. 'An admirable ending to a meal', in the words of cookery writer Ambrose Heath (who devoted a whole tome, *Good Savouries,* to the topic), 'like some unexpected witticism or amusing epigram at the close of a pleasant conversation'.

But although these grand, rather heavy dinners have their place, these days it's all a bit of an effort. More important still, tastes have changed and our tender modern tummies (well, most of them) just wouldn't, er, stomach it. But that doesn't mean the savoury has to go the way of turtle soup. Hell no! These bold, brusque and vibrant flavours are timeless, with cheese, anchovy, cured pork and cayenne pepper all leading players in this delectable cavalcade. Toast, preferably thin, buttered and piping hot, was the base upon which all manner of gastronomic greatness could be balanced. Plus tartlets, croûtes, biscuits and puff pastry barquettes.

For me, one of the many joys of the savoury is that they're welcome at any time of the day – mid-morning snack, light lunch, ballast for booze, easy supper, late-night nibble. Even, if your tastes are that way inclined, as a canapé. Devilled sardines, to name but one, are not only economical but taste wonderful too. Plus they can be put together with the most basic of store-cupboard ingredients – emergency fallbacks that don't reek of desperation, giving the time-poor cook the vestige of old-school sophistication. Cheese on toast is one thing. Mix that cheese with a little beer, though, and let it bubble and seethe and brown, and the whole thing becomes Welsh Rarebit, a dish that Fortnum's might not have invented. But one that they certainly perfected.

Okay, no one (save the ghost of Fanny Cradock) is going to whip up exotic vol-au-vents on a daily basis. These particular beauties are best saved for a slower, more rainy day. But don't fear this rambunctious taste of days long past. I'm still stirred by the sight of a savoury, peeking out bravely after the assault of pudding. Treat them as endlessly adaptable, and the savoury moves from dinner delectation to anytime delight.

Canapés Ivanhoe

Not actually a canapé, but a savoury. Smoked haddock, cooked in white wine and cream, served atop a baked mushroom. I'm not sure what it has to do with Sir Walter Scott's Norman knight, save being reassuringly solid, noble and reliable. Serve as a snack or savoury. Or a late-night feast.

Serves 4

4 medium-sized flat mushrooms
olive oil, for drizzling
4 sprigs of thyme
20g unsalted butter
250g undyed smoked haddock, skinned and cut into 1cm dice
2 tablespoons white wine
100ml double cream
a pinch of cayenne pepper
a squeeze of lemon juice
1½ tablespoons chopped flat-leaf parsley
4 slices of brown or sourdough bread, toasted
salt and freshly ground black pepper

Peel the flat mushrooms, discarding the stalks, and place them on a baking sheet. Drizzle with olive oil, season with salt and pepper and sprinkle with the leaves from the thyme sprigs. Place in an oven heated to 180°C/Gas Mark 4 and cook for 8 minutes, until the mushrooms are tender. Remove from the oven and set aside.

Melt the butter in a pan, add the diced haddock and cook gently until it turns white. Add the white wine and simmer until almost completely evaporated. Add the double cream, cayenne pepper and some black pepper and simmer for 5–6 minutes, until the cream has reduced enough to coat the haddock lightly. Add a squeeze of lemon juice, check the seasoning and stir in a tablespoon of the chopped parsley.

Put the toast on 4 serving plates. Top each slice with a mushroom, fill it with the smoked haddock mixture and sprinkle with the remaining parsley.

Welsh Rarebit

Rarebit? Rabbit? Rarerabbit? The argument as to correct spelling and pronunciation burns eternal, but all that really matters is Cheddar cheese, mixed with mustard, Worcestershire sauce, a whole egg and a drop of beer. Fortnum's use Guinness, although any stout or bitter will do fine. This is then slathered over good toast, grilled until bubbling and finished with half a grilled tomato and a shake of Worcestershire sauce. One customer is so enamoured by the dish that whenever he flies in from Santa Barbara, California, he dumps his bags at the Stafford Hotel and rushes over the road for rarebit. Without even checking in. Done well, this dish inspires that sort of devotion.

Serves 4

4 slices of brown or sourdough bread
2 tomatoes, cut in half
sea salt and coarsely ground black pepper

For the rarebit mix
4 teaspoons Guinness
1 teaspoon English mustard
½ teaspoon Worcestershire sauce
a few drops of Tabasco sauce
1 egg
250g mature Cheddar cheese, grated

To make the rarebit mix, combine the Guinness, mustard, Worcestershire sauce, Tabasco and egg in a bowl. Add the grated cheese and mix well. Lightly toast the sourdough bread and spread the rarebit mixture on top. Place under a hot grill until golden brown, then transfer to an oven heated to 180°C/Gas Mark 4 and bake for 3 minutes.

Meanwhile, put the tomato halves under the hot grill until lightly browned. Serve each slice of rarebit sprinkled with sea salt and coarsely ground black pepper and accompanied by a tomato half.

Scotch Woodcock

A classic, rich savoury, with a classic English joke attached. The Scots have long been famed for their parsimony – by their neighbours south of the border, anyway. Hence 'Scotch' woodcock, implying that they're too mean to use the game bird and swap it for far cheaper anchovy paste. A fairly poor joke actually makes a fairly rich dish.

Serves 2

5 eggs, preferably Burford Browns
50ml double cream
a pinch of cayenne pepper
1 teaspoon anchovy essence or anchovy paste
30g unsalted butter
2 slices of sourdough bread
6 thin anchovy fillets
salt and freshly ground black pepper

Crack the eggs into a bowl, add the double cream, cayenne pepper, anchovy essence or paste and some salt and pepper and whisk together. Melt the butter in a non-stick pan and add the egg mixture. Cook very gently, mixing with a spatula, until softly scrambled.

Toast the bread and place on 2 serving plates. Top with the scrambled egg and lay the anchovy fillets on top. Eat, and marvel at its salty, savoury depth.

Angels on Horseback

'The finest savoury of all', in the words of Ambrose Heath (a cookery writer of the early twentieth century) and a gentlemen's-clubland classic that broke out of St. James. Oysters (use rocks, as their flavour is less delicate), wrapped in bacon, are simply grilled or roasted on skewers.

Makes 12

6 rashers of smoked streaky bacon
12 rock oysters, shucked

Soak two 12cm-long bamboo skewers in water for about 30 minutes.

Cut each streaky bacon rasher in half. Place an oyster on top of each half and wrap it up in the bacon. Thread the rolls on to the skewers.

Place in an oven heated to 220°C/Gas Mark 7 and bake for 8–10 minutes, until the bacon is crisp and the oysters are plump (alternatively you could cook them under a hot grill, as is traditional). Discard the skewers and serve immediately – on hot buttered toast, if you like.

Wild Mushroom and Spinach Vol-au-vents with Madeira Cream Sauce

Life, to paraphrase Shirley Conran, is too short to stuff a vol-au-vent. In most cases, they really are the most ridiculous confection, a sort of edible Hyacinth Bouquet, the teacup-raised pinkie made real. Sodden, sullen pastry, filled with some sort of turgid beige concoction.

But the Fortnum's vol-au-vent is, of course, something altogether more noble. Blessed with retro charm. Frilly, burnished, gently buttery puff pastry enclosing the choicest, creamiest morsels of wild mushrooms, spinach and goat's cheese. Vol-au-vents. But not as we know 'em.

Makes 6

500g good-quality bought puff pastry
flour, for dusting
1 egg yolk, lightly beaten
salt and freshly ground black pepper

For the spinach filling
500g spinach
125g soft fresh goat's cheese

For the wild mushroom filling
500g wild mushrooms
2 tablespoons olive oil
1 shallot, finely chopped
2 garlic cloves, finely chopped
60ml white wine
1 tablespoon chopped tarragon

For the Madeira cream sauce
1 tablespoon olive oil
1 shallot, finely chopped
1 garlic clove, finely chopped
250g wild mushrooms
100ml Madeira
250ml double cream
1 tablespoon chopped tarragon

On a work surface dusted with flour, roll out the pastry to about 4mm thick. Cut out 12 discs with a 10cm pastry cutter. Using a 6.5cm cutter, cut out a circle of pastry from the centre of half the discs and discard. Brush the 6 whole circles with egg yolk and place on a baking sheet lined with baking parchment. Place the pastry rings on top and brush those with egg yolk too. Chill while you prepare the fillings.

Remove any large stalks from the spinach and wash it well. Drain, then put into a large saucepan with just the water clinging to its leaves. Cover and cook over a medium heat for 2–3 minutes, until wilted. Gently squeeze out excess liquid, then return the spinach to the pan, season well with salt and pepper and stir in the goat's cheese.

To make the mushroom filling, trim the mushrooms and cut them into halves or quarters, depending on their size. Heat the oil in a large frying pan, add the shallot and garlic and cook for 3 minutes, until softened. Add the mushrooms and some salt and pepper and cook until the mushrooms are tender. Pour in the white wine and simmer until almost completely evaporated, then remove the pan from the heat and set aside.

Remove the vol-au-vent cases from the fridge and place in an oven heated to 180°C/Gas Mark 4. Cook for 15–20 minutes, until they are a rich golden brown and the pastry is cooked all the way through. If the centre has puffed up, gently deflate it with a fork.

While the pastry is cooking, make the sauce. Heat the olive oil in a large pan, add the shallot and garlic and cook for 3 minutes, until softened. Cut up the mushrooms, add them to the pan with some salt and pepper and cook for about 3–4 minutes, until just tender. Pour in the Madeira and simmer until it has reduced by half. Add the double cream, bring to the boil and simmer for 5 minutes. Using an electric handheld blender, purée the sauce until smooth. Stir in the tarragon.

Quickly reheat the spinach filling and the wild mushrooms, adding the tarragon to the mushrooms. Fill the pastry cases half full with the spinach, then top up with the wild mushrooms. Serve immediately, with the sauce on the side.

Pea Panna Cotta with Cheese Straws and Quail's Eggs

A savoury panna cotta, I hear you cry? What would the Italians say? But this is suitably wobbling and verdant, and looks a lot more difficult to cook than it actually is. You could also serve it as a canapé, or as a starter, for four, in Martini glasses. The cheese straws are easy to make too, and you're left with rather more than you need. Perks of the chef and all that. You could replace half the Parmesan with Gruyère or Comté for more of an Alpine feel.

Serves 8

1 gelatine leaf
170g fresh peas
260g frozen peas
leaves from 2 sprigs of mint
110ml double cream
1 large egg yolk
4 quail's eggs
salt and freshly ground black pepper

For the cheese straws
100g good-quality bought puff pastry
flour, for dusting
1 egg yolk, lightly beaten, to glaze
25g Parmesan cheese, grated

Put the gelatine into a dish of cold water and leave to soak for about 5 minutes. Put the fresh and frozen peas into a pan with the mint, cream and some salt and pepper and bring to the boil. Simmer for a minute or so, until the peas are tender, then transfer the mixture to a blender or food processor and blend until smooth. Remove 4 teaspoons of the mixture and set aside. Mix the egg yolk into the remaining mixture, then pass through a sieve into a clean pan and reheat gently. Lift the gelatine out of the water and gently squeeze out the excess liquid. Add the gelatine to the pea mixture and stir until dissolved.

Pour the pea purée into 8 shot glasses and leave in the fridge to set.

To make the cheese straws, roll the puff pastry out on a floured surface into a rectangle, then cut it in half to make 2 squares. Brush one piece with the egg yolk and sprinkle with the Parmesan cheese. Cover with the other piece of puff pastry and press down to make sure the pieces stick together. Chill for 20 minutes, then cut into 12 sticks. Twist each stick to make a spiral and put on a baking tray lined with baking parchment. Chill for another 10 minutes, then place in an oven heated to 180°C/Gas Mark 4 and bake for 10–12 minutes, until the cheese straws are golden.

Put the quail's eggs into a pan of gently simmering water and boil for 1½ minutes; this should give soft-boiled eggs. Cool them under running water, then peel them. Top each pea panna cotta with ½ teaspoon of the reserved pea purée and lean a quail's egg against it. Serve with a cheese straw.

Dinner

‘Dine light-heartedly, and rely on Fortnum’s’

Scallops in the Half Shell with Duchesse Potatoes and Champagne Sauce

Plump shellfish, sweet as spring water, surrounded by soft waves of Champagne, butter, and shallot-infused mashed potato. What's not to love? Forget those insipid 70s disasters, with cheap, rubbery scallops and an excess of fake Cheddar cheese. This is a classic, and best served, of course, in the original scallop shell. Retro? Perhaps. But there's no doubting its eternal appeal.

Serves 4

80g unsalted butter
1 small carrot, cut into small matchsticks
1 small leek, cut into small matchsticks
1 small courgette, cut into small matchsticks
1 banana shallot, finely diced
1 bay leaf
100ml Champagne
200ml double cream
8 diver-caught scallops on the half shell, roes removed
1 tablespoon chopped chives
sea salt and freshly ground white pepper

For the duchesse potatoes
1 large baking potato
20g unsalted butter, melted
1 egg yolk

For the duchesse potatoes, wrap the potato in foil, place it in an oven heated to 200°C/Gas Mark 6 and bake until tender. Scoop out the flesh and push it through a potato ricer or a sieve into a bowl. Mix in the melted butter and season well. When the potato is warm rather than hot, beat in the egg yolk, transfer the mixture to a piping bag fitted with a star nozzle and set aside.

Heat 30g of the butter in a small pan, add the carrot, leek and courgette and cook over a low heat until tender. Season with salt and pepper, then remove from the heat and set aside.

Melt 30g of the remaining butter in a small saucepan, add the shallot and cook until soft but not coloured. Add the bay leaf, then the Champagne, and simmer until the Champagne has reduced by half. Pour in the double cream and reduce by half again, then season well. Remove from the heat and keep warm.

Remove the scallops from their shells, then wash and dry the shells. Pipe the duchesse mix around the edge of each one in a curly pattern, creating a nest. Place the shells on a baking tray and glaze the potato under a hot grill.

Pat the scallops dry and season them well. Heat the remaining butter in a heavy-based frying pan, then add the scallops and sear them for a minute or so on each side, until lightly golden brown.

Put the scallop shells on 4 serving plates (you can pipe a little of the remaining duchesse potato in the centre of each plate, if you like, to hold the shells in place). Place a spoonful of the vegetable strips in each shell and put 2 scallops on top. Cover with the Champagne sauce and sprinkle with the chives.

Blanquette of Veal with Spring Vegetables

This is all about a whiter shade of pale, a classic bourgeois ragoût of pale meat, sauce and white pepper. A light spring dish, it was originally sold in tins at Fortnum's, made on the premises. Serve with baby vegetables and steamed rice.

Serves 4–6

1kg leg of rose veal, cut into 4cm cubes
1 bay leaf, 2 thyme sprigs and some parsley stalks, tied into a bouquet garni with string
1 onion, roughly chopped
1 carrot, roughly chopped
1 celery stalk, roughly chopped
2 litres light chicken stock
50g unsalted butter
4 tablespoons plain flour
100ml double cream
lemon juice (optional)
4 tablespoons chopped flat-leaf parsley
salt and freshly ground white pepper

For the spring vegetables
300g button onions
40g unsalted butter
a bunch of baby carrots
a bunch of baby leeks
a bunch of baby fennel or baby courgettes

Put the diced veal into a large pan, cover with plenty of cold water, then add a pinch of salt. Bring to a simmer and cook gently for 5 minutes; this will help remove any blood and impurities from the veal. Drain under cold water, then place in a clean pan. Add the bouquet garni, onion, carrot and celery, pour over the chicken stock and bring to a simmer. Cook very gently for 1½–2 hours, until the veal is tender.

Meanwhile, peel the button onions, put them into a pan of boiling salted water, and cook for about 5 minutes, until almost tender. Drain well, refresh under cold running water, then drain again. Melt 20g of the butter in a small frying pan, then add the onions and cook gently, without letting them colour, until they are silky and glazed with the butter. Remove from the heat and set aside.

Blanch the baby vegetables separately in a large pan of boiling salted water until just tender, lifting them out with a slotted spoon as they are done and adding the next batch. Refresh immediately in cold water, then drain and pat dry. Set aside.

Once the veal is tender, strain off the stock into a separate pan. Pick the vegetables and bouquet garni out from among the veal and discard. Simmer the stock until reduced to about 750ml.

Melt the butter in the pan in which you cooked the veal, then stir in the flour to make a roux and cook gently for 1 minute. Gradually add the hot stock, stirring constantly to give a smooth sauce. When all the stock has been added, bring to a simmer and cook for 5 minutes. The sauce should have the consistency of pouring cream.

Stir in the double cream and season to taste with salt and pepper. Return the veal to the pan with the baby onions and heat through gently for 5–10 minutes. Meanwhile, melt the remaining 20g butter in a frying pan, add the baby vegetables and heat through gently. Season to taste.

To serve, check the seasoning of the blanquette, adding a few drops of lemon juice, if you like. Place the veal in shallow bowls and pour the sauce around. Top with the baby vegetables and sprinkle with the parsley. Serve with a rice pilaff.

Skate au Poivre

No, not a typo, rather cartilaginous ray, cooked with the classic pepper sauce. The soft flesh has a robust flavour and holds up well to all that creamy pungency. Crack the pepper in a pestle and mortar and apply liberally.

Serve with Braised Baby Gems with Orange and Star Anise (see page 217).

Serves 2

2 skate wings, weighing about 200g each
2 tablespoons olive oil
20g unsalted butter
2 tablespoons chopped flat-leaf parsley
salt and coarsely cracked black pepper

For the sauce
30g unsalted butter
1 banana shallot, finely diced
1 teaspoon coarsely cracked black pepper
40ml brandy
100ml white wine
150ml chicken stock
50ml double cream

First make the sauce. Heat the butter in a small pan, add the shallot and cracked black pepper and cook until the shallot is tender. Add the brandy, heat for a few seconds, then set it alight, standing well back. When the flames have died away, add the white wine and simmer until reduced by about three-quarters. Add the chicken stock and simmer until reduced by half. Finally add the double cream and simmer until the sauce has reduced to a coating consistency. Taste and adjust the seasoning if necessary.

Season the skate wings well with salt and coarsely cracked black pepper. Heat the olive oil and butter in a heavy-based frying pan that is large enough to hold the skate. Add the fish to the pan and fry for 4–5 minutes on each side, until the flesh parts easily from the bone when a knife is inserted.

Serve the skate coated with the pepper sauce and sprinkled with the chopped parsley.

Goan Fish Curry

A new addition to the menu at 45 Jermyn St., this takes an ugly fish and turns its toothsomely textured tail into an elegantly spiced curry. Spices were one of the foundations upon which Fortnum's was built, along with tea, coffee and honey. Here, a classic collection of South Indian spices are used to create a pure Goan delight.

Serves 6

6 portions of monkfish tail, on the bone
a splash of vegetable oil
300g shallots, finely diced
½ teaspoon ground turmeric
1½ teaspoons each of garam masala, ground cumin, ground coriander
250g tomatoes, skinned and diced (seeds included)
salt and freshly ground black pepper
chopped coriander, to garnish

For the marinade
1½ teaspoons chilli powder
1½ teaspoons turmeric
juice of 1 lemon
50ml vegetable oil

For the purée
50g tamarind paste
200g shallots, chopped
200g tomatoes, skinned and diced (seeds included)
20g fresh ginger, chopped
2 garlic cloves, chopped
2 green chillies, deseeded and chopped
1½ teaspoons each of garam masala, ground fenugreek, ground turmeric, ground cumin, ground coriander
2 x 400ml tins of coconut milk

For the tarka (tempering)
75ml vegetable oil
1 teaspoon black mustard seeds
1 teaspoon fenugreek seeds
8 curry leaves
1 tablespoon finely chopped garlic
100g red onion, finely chopped

Skin the monkfish tails, if your fishmonger hasn't already done so, and cut them in half. Mix together all the ingredients for the marinade, season with salt and pepper, then add the monkfish and leave to marinate for 2 hours.

Put all the ingredients for the purée in a blender or food processor and whiz until smooth.

Heat the vegetable oil in a large frying pan. Add the monkfish and cook briefly until sealed all over, then remove from the pan and set aside. Add the diced shallots to the pan and cook until lightly browned. Stir in the turmeric, garam masala, cumin and coriander and cook for 2 minutes. Add the tomatoes and bring to a simmer, stirring to deglaze the pan. Add the purée, season with salt and bring back to a simmer. Cook for 3–4 minutes.

Meanwhile, in a separate pan, heat the oil for the tarka until almost smoking. Quickly add the mustard and fenugreek seeds and stand back while they pop. After a few seconds, add the curry leaves, garlic and red onion. Cook for 30 seconds, then pour everything, including the oil, into the main sauce.

Return the monkfish to the pan, then cover and cook gently for about 4 minutes until the fish is cooked through. Scatter with chopped coriander and serve with rice.

Sea Trout en Croute with Chive Butter Sauce and Tenderstem Broccoli

This recipe uses individual portions of sea trout, that magnificent spring and early summer fish. But salmon will do just fine. The dish is made even better by the fish being wrapped first in spinach, then a pancake, then in the pastry. A triple hit, if you will, of texture and flavour. These can be prepared well in advance and baked just before serving.

Serves 4

25g large spinach leaves
4 x 70g thick rectangles of sea trout fillet, skin off
1 egg yolk, lightly beaten
225g good-quality puff pastry
350g tenderstem broccoli
30g unsalted butter
salt and freshly ground black pepper

For the pancakes
100g plain flour
a small pinch each of salt and sugar
2 eggs
200ml milk
2 tablespoons chopped chives
a little butter, for frying

For the chive butter sauce
2 banana shallots, finely diced
1 garlic clove, crushed
4 sprigs of thyme
50ml white wine
50ml white wine vinegar
50ml double cream
200g cold unsalted butter, cut into cubes
juice of ½ lemon
2 tablespoons chopped chives

First make the pancakes. Sift the flour into a bowl, add the salt and sugar and make a well in the centre. Add the eggs to the well and beat with a wooden spoon, gradually drawing in the flour from the sides. Slowly add the milk, beating until you have a smooth, thin batter with a few small bubbles on the surface. Mix in the chives.

Place a pancake pan or a medium frying pan over a moderate heat and grease with a little butter. Add enough of the pancake batter to make a thin pancake, swirling it around the pan so it covers the base evenly. Cook for 1–2 minutes, until golden underneath, then turn and cook the other side. Turn out of the pan on to a piece of baking parchment and cook the remaining batter in the same way. The pancakes can be stacked on top of each other once cooked. (You will have more pancakes than you need, so either stop after you've made 4 and store the batter in the fridge for the next day, or treat yourself to the extra ones.)

Remove any large stalks from the spinach leaves. Blanch the leaves for 10 seconds in a large pan of boiling salted water, then drain and immediately place under cold running water to stop the cooking. When the spinach is cool, gently press out the excess water and lay the leaves out on a tea towel to dry.

Place a piece of cling film on the work surface and put a pancake on top. Place a spinach leaf on top of that, then a piece of sea trout. Season the fish well with salt and pepper. Wrap the spinach around the fish so it is fully covered. Brush one end of the pancake with some of the beaten egg yolk and wrap the trout up, ensuring the sides of the pancake are tucked in and the end sticks to the egg (it should look like a large spring roll). Roll the whole thing up tightly in the cling film, taking care to keep the rectangular shape. Repeat with the remaining ingredients.

Cut the puff pastry into quarters. On a lightly floured work surface, roll out each piece quite thinly, so it is large enough to enclose a sea trout parcel, then run a lattice cutter over it. Brush all over with the remaining beaten egg yolk. Remove the cling film from the fish parcels and wrap them in the pastry, pinching the ends together to seal. Brush the top with egg yolk and place the parcels in the fridge while you start on the chive butter sauce.

Put the shallots, garlic, thyme, white wine and white wine vinegar in a pan and simmer for 5–10 minutes, until the liquid has reduced to a glaze. Add the cream and simmer until reduced by half. Turn the heat down as low as it will go and quickly whisk in the butter a few pieces at a time until you have a smooth, emulsified sauce – lift the pan off the heat occasionally as you do this, so the sauce doesn't overheat. Add the lemon juice and chives and keep warm.

Place the fish parcels in an oven heated to 190°C/ Gas Mark 5 and bake for 10–15 minutes, until golden brown. Meanwhile, cook the broccoli in boiling salted water for 3–4 minutes, until tender. Drain well, then return to the pan and toss with the butter. Season to taste.

To serve, trim the ends off the fish parcels and cut each one in half. Divide the broccoli between 4 plates and place the parcels on top, fish side facing up. Pour a little of the sauce around and serve the rest in a jug on the side.

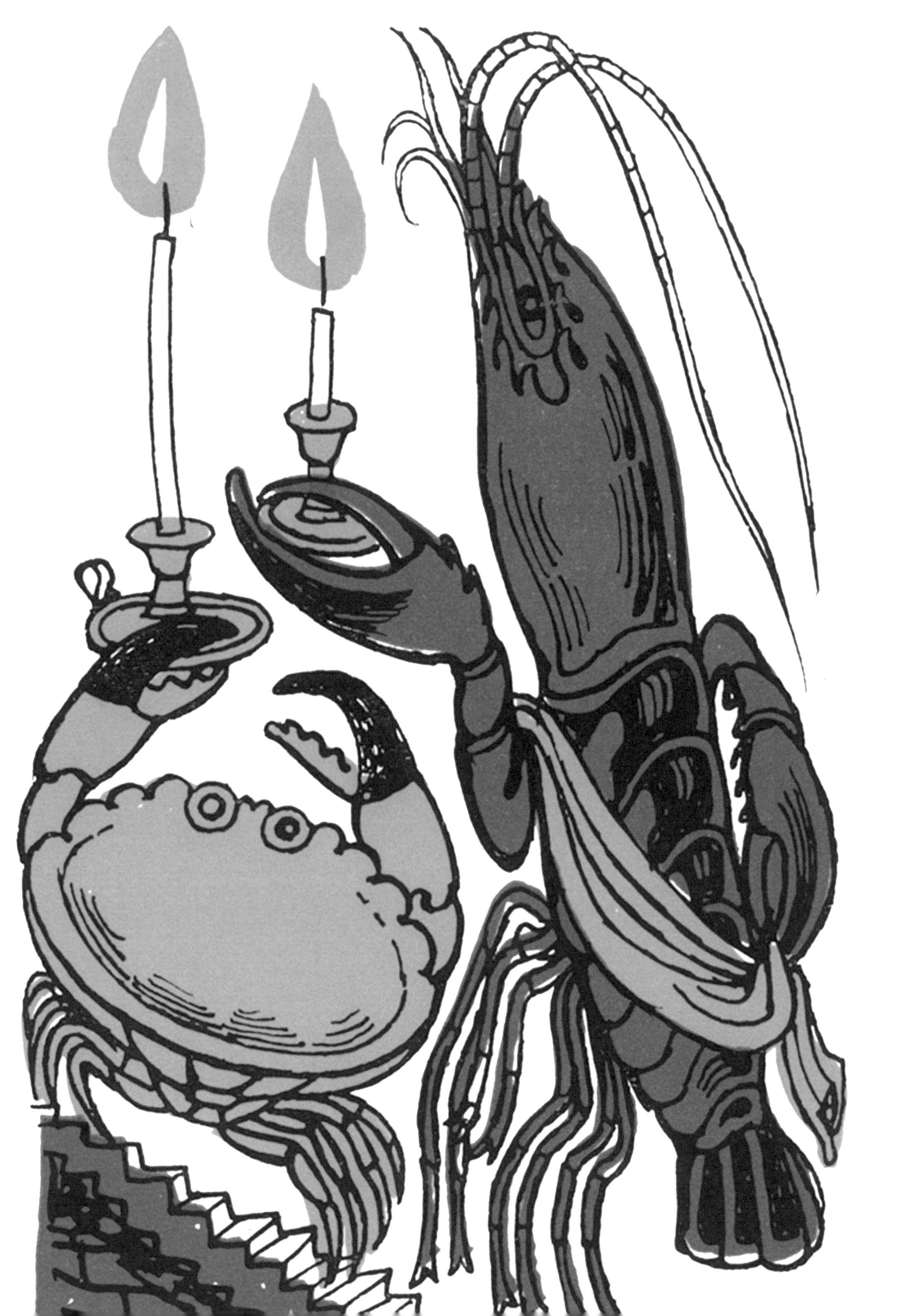

Braised Ox Cheek with Horseradish Mash

Ox cheek – all that chewing of cud makes it a tough cut. But slow-cooked it softens splendidly. Marinate the meat in red wine with mixed vegetables the day before. And you can use hot horseradish cream in your mash, although fresh packs more punch. Just buy a root, grate, and add with a generous (but not too generous) hand. You will probably need to order the ox cheek in advance and make sure the butcher trims it well.

Serves 4

1kg ox cheek, trimmed and chopped into pieces
400g carrots, chopped
2 leeks, sliced
4 celery stalks, sliced
600ml red wine
4 tablespoons vegetable oil
1 litre beef/veal stock
a small bunch of thyme
2 bay leaves
1–2 teaspoons redcurrant jelly
40g unsalted butter, diced
2 tablespoons chopped flat-leaf parsley
salt and freshly ground black pepper

For the horseradish mash
4 large, floury potatoes, such as Maris Piper, cut into chunks
50g unsalted butter
50ml double cream
50ml milk
1 heaped tablespoon creamed horseradish

Put the ox cheek in a dish with the carrots, leeks and celery. Add the wine, cover and leave to marinate in the fridge overnight.

The next day, strain the meat and vegetables, reserving the wine. Heat half the vegetable oil in a large, heavy-based frying pan and seal the ox cheek in batches, transferring it to a casserole as it is done. Pour the wine and stock into the pan and bring to the boil, stirring and scraping the base of the pan with a wooden spoon to deglaze it, then add it to the meat in the casserole.

Heat the remaining oil in the frying pan and sauté the vegetables from the marinade. Add them to the casserole, together with the thyme and bay leaves. Bring to a simmer, season well, then cover and transfer to an oven heated to 140°C/Gas Mark 1. Braise for 3 hours, until the meat is tender. The top of the ox cheek should be very soft to the touch and may seem overcooked, but when it cools the structure will reset itself.

Strain off the sauce into a clean pan and simmer until it has reduced by about half; it should have a thin coating consistency. Stir in redcurrant jelly to taste, then whisk in the butter a few pieces at a time to give a glossy sauce. Keep warm.

For the horseradish mash, cook the potatoes in boiling salted water until tender, then drain well. Gently heat the butter, cream and milk in the pan, then return the potatoes to it and mash thoroughly. Mix in the creamed horseradish and season to taste.

Divide the mash between individual plates, add the ox cheek and pour the sauce over and around. Sprinkle with the chopped parsley.

Deep-fried Courgette Flowers with Graceburn Cheese and Honey

Courgette flowers bloom from mid-spring to mid-summer. At Fortnum's, the flowers are grown on the roof, and are drizzled with honey taken from their own rooftop hives. Fortnum's use Graceburn London goat's cheese, but any light variety will work.

As anyone who has grown courgettes knows well, they spread like triffids. Just pick the flowers gently, still attached to the courgette, and use immediately.

Serves 4

8 courgette flowers, with small courgettes attached
200g Graceburn cheese
vegetable oil, for deep-frying
50g plain flour
sea salt
good-quality runny honey, to serve

For the batter
200g tempura flour
about 250ml sparkling water

Carefully open the courgette flowers, taking care not to tear the petals. There will be a small stamen inside each one. Twist it and carefully pull it out. Blend the Graceburn cheese in a food processor until it is slightly whipped. Either pipe or spoon it into the courgette flowers. Gently close the flowers, twisting the ends together to seal.

To make the batter, put the tempura flour into a bowl and whisk in the sparkling water a little at a time until you have a smooth mixture with no lumps.

Heat the vegetable oil to 180°C in a deep-fat fryer or a large, deep saucepan (if you use a saucepan, don't fill it more than a third full, or you risk it boiling over). Meanwhile, put the flour in a shallow dish and coat the stuffed courgettes in it, gently shaking off the excess. Now dip the flowers into the batter, ensuring everything is completely covered. Fry them 2 or 3 at a time for about 3 minutes, until golden brown and crisp.

Drain on kitchen paper and sprinkle with salt. Divide between 4 serving plates and drizzle with a little honey. Serve with a heritage tomato and shallot salad.

Vegetarian Chole Curry

This is a beautifully spiced North Indian chickpea curry, which not only draws upon Fortnum's long heritage of spice (they were selling them way before they became common culinary parlance), but caters to an ever-increasing hunger for healthy vegetarian dishes.

Cinnamon, cardamom, cumin, chilli and coriander seeds all meld to create a simple dish with endlessly exotic allure. Try to roast and grind your spices fresh, so all those lovely oils dance and dart about the tongue.

Serves 6

300g dried chickpeas, soaked in plenty of cold water overnight
2 breakfast-blend tea bags
1 black cardamom pod
2 large onions
3 tablespoons ghee
1 tablespoon cumin seeds
6 cloves
1 green cardamom pod
2 cinnamon sticks
2 bay leaves
1 tablespoon ginger paste
1 tablespoon garlic paste
2.5cm piece of fresh ginger, finely chopped
1 teaspoon ground white pepper
1 teaspoon ground fennel seeds
1 teaspoon ground cumin
1 teaspoon ground coriander
1 teaspoon ground turmeric
1 tablespoon red chilli powder
1 tablespoon anardana (pomegranate seed) powder (optional)
1 teaspoon tomato purée
400g tin of chopped tomatoes
500ml water
½ bunch of coriander
juice of ½ lime
1 teaspoon amchur (dried mango powder)
salt

Drain the soaked chickpeas, then put them into a pan, cover with plenty of fresh water and add the tea bags and the black cardamom. Bring to the boil and simmer for about 50–60 minutes, until tender. Discard the tea bags, then drain the chickpeas and set aside (you can leave the black cardamom pod in with the chickpeas).

Peel and roughly chop the onions, then whiz them to a coarse paste in a food processor. Heat the ghee in a large pan, add the cumin seeds, cloves, green cardamom, cinnamon sticks and bay leaves and sauté over a medium heat for 20 seconds. Stir in the ginger and garlic pastes and the chopped fresh ginger and sauté for a few seconds longer. Add the onions and cook gently for 8–10 minutes, until softened but not coloured.

Mix together the ground white pepper, fennel seeds, cumin, coriander, turmeric, red chilli powder and the anardana, if you have it. Add to the onion mixture and cook, stirring, over a medium heat for 2–3 minutes. Stir in the tomato purée, followed by the tinned tomatoes, and continue to stir for 3–4 minutes longer. Add the chickpeas and the water, bring to a simmer and cook for about 30 minutes, until the sauce is thick.

Chop the coriander leaves and stalks (a lot of the flavour is in the stalks) and stir them into the curry, together with the lime juice and amchur. Taste and add salt if necessary. Serve with basmati rice.

Baked White Onion with Courgette

Baked onion, cooked until it almost collapses, has been a long-standing favourite on Fortnum's menus. Here, the recipe has been modernised, using courgettes grown on the roof, and English shiitake mushrooms from Cornwall. A dish to convert even the most fervent of carnivores.

Serves 2

2 large white onions
60g unsalted butter
1 yellow and 1 green courgette (about 360g total weight)
1 large bunch of spring onions, chopped
2 garlic cloves, chopped
60g shiitake mushrooms, sliced
15g fresh breadcrumbs
20g Parmesan cheese, grated, plus extra to serve
salt and freshly ground black pepper

For the sauce
25g unsalted butter
1 shallot, finely diced
50ml white wine
50ml double cream
1 tablespoon finely chopped flat-leaf parsley

Peel each onion, slice off the top and trim the roots, leaving the base intact. Grease a small, deep casserole with 20g of the butter, put the onions in it with 120ml water and some salt and pepper, then cover tightly. Place in an oven heated to 160°C/ Gas Mark 3 and bake for about 50 minutes, until the onions are tender but still holding their shape. Remove from the oven and leave to cool. Carefully remove the inner layers of onion, leaving the outer layers intact. Finely chop the inner layers.

Trim the courgettes and cut each one lengthwise in half. Cut one half of each courgette into batons and blanch in boiling salted water for 1 minute. Drain and set aside. Finely dice the rest of each courgette.

Heat 30g of the remaining butter in a pan, add the spring onions and garlic and cook until soft. Add the sliced shiitake mushrooms and the diced courgette and cook until softened but not coloured. Stir in the chopped onion, followed by the breadcrumbs and Parmesan. Season to taste. Fill the onion shells with this mixture, setting aside any excess. Sprinkle with extra Parmesan and return to the oven. Cook at 180°C/Gas Mark 4 for 8–10 minutes, until thoroughly heated through.

For the sauce, melt the butter in a small pan, add the shallot and cook until soft. Add the white wine and simmer until almost completely evaporated. Pour in the double cream and bring to a simmer, then stir in the parsley and some seasoning.

Reheat the blanched courgettes in the remaining 10g of butter and season to taste.

To serve, place any extra filling in the middle of each plate, top with the yellow and green courgette batons and add a baked onion to the side. Pour a thin thread of sauce around each plate.

Chicken with Squash

The joy of this dish, taken from the 45 Jermyn St. menu, lies in its simplicity. The spiced relish can be made in advance and kept in the fridge until ready to use. Then all you need do is cook the breast and fennel. And in 20 minutes, you have a serious dinner. Goosnargh chicken is one of the finest birds you'll ever taste. Well worth seeking out. And the Chardonnay vinegar adds splendid zing.

Serves 4

4 fennel bulbs
4 chicken breasts, skin on
80ml rapeseed oil
salt and freshly ground black pepper

For the butternut squash relish
4 tablespoons olive oil
2 shallots, finely diced
1 red chilli, deseeded and finely diced
400g butternut squash, cut into 1cm cubes
2 teaspoons fennel seeds, roughly crushed
4 tablespoons Chardonnay vinegar (if you cannot get Chardonnay vinegar, substitute good-quality white wine vinegar and 2 teaspoons sugar)
20g pumpkin seeds, lightly toasted in a dry frying pan
2 tablespoons chopped flat-leaf parsley

First make the relish. Heat the olive oil in a frying pan, then add the shallots and chilli and fry for about 5 minutes, until softened but not coloured. Add the butternut squash cubes and fennel seeds and fry for a couple of minutes longer, then cover the pan and cook for 15 minutes or until the squash is just tender but still holding its shape. Add the vinegar, raise the heat a little and simmer until reduced by about two-thirds. Taste and adjust the seasoning, then leave to cool. Stir in the pumpkin seeds and flat-leaf parsley, plus a drizzle of olive oil, if you like.

Trim the fennel bulbs and cut them into quarters if small, eighths if large, making sure the pieces stay attached at the root end. Season the chicken breasts with salt and pepper. Heat the rapeseed oil in a heavy-based frying pan, add the chicken breasts, skin side down, and cook over a medium heat until golden brown underneath. Turn them over and transfer them to a small roasting tin. Place them in an oven heated to 180°C/Gas Mark 4 and cook for about 15 minutes, until there is no pinkness inside when you insert a knife.

Meanwhile, add the fennel pieces to the pan in which the chicken was browned and cook over a low to medium heat, turning every 5 minutes, until they are golden and tender. Season to taste.

Serve the chicken accompanied by the fennel pieces and the butternut squash relish.

Chicken Chasseur

What sins have been visited upon this blameless 'hunter's chicken' dish over the years, taking it from sophisticated luncheon to mid-80s nouvelle cuisine catastrophe. But this is the proper recipe, simple and classic, always popular in Fortnum's. Use a chicken supreme (a breast with skin and wing attached). If not available, breasts are fine.

Serves 2

2 corn-fed chicken supremes (i.e. the breasts, skin-on, with the wing bone attached)
1 tablespoon olive oil
salt and freshly ground black pepper

For the sauce
50g unsalted butter
1 shallot, finely diced
2 garlic cloves, finely diced
2 plum tomatoes, skinned, deseeded and diced
a pinch of sugar
100ml white wine
500ml chicken stock
120g button mushrooms, halved
1 tablespoon chopped tarragon

For the mashed potato
300g floury potatoes, such as Maris Piper
50g unsalted butter
25ml double cream

Wrap the potatoes individually in foil and bake them at 200°C/Gas Mark 6 for about an hour, until they are soft all the way through when pierced with a knife. When they are done, heat the butter and cream in a saucepan until the butter melts. Cut the potatoes in half and scoop out the flesh. Push it through a potato ricer or a sieve into the butter and cream and beat with a wooden spoon until smooth. Season to taste.

Season the chicken. Heat the oil in an ovenproof frying pan, add the chicken breasts, skin side down, and fry until golden. Turn them over and transfer the pan to an oven heated to 180°C/Gas Mark 4. Cook for 10–12 minutes, until the juices run clear when a knife is inserted near the bone. Leave to rest in a warm place for 5 minutes.

While the chicken is cooking, prepare the sauce. Heat 20g of the butter in a pan, add the shallot and garlic and cook gently until soft. Stir in the tomatoes and cook for 5 minutes, then add the sugar (this will help ensure the sauce is not too acidic) and pour in the wine. Boil until the wine has almost completely evaporated. Add the chicken stock and boil until reduced by half. Blitz the sauce with a handheld electric blender until smooth.

Add the mushrooms to the sauce and simmer for 5 minutes. Finish the sauce with the chopped tarragon leaves and whisk in the remaining butter to get a good glossy finish. Season to taste.

Place the mash in the centre of 2 shallow serving bowls and place the chicken breasts on top. Finish with the sauce spooned over and around.

Lamb Cutlets with Redcurrant and Mint Glaze

A long-time customer recently visited the store, in search of his beloved cutlets glacé. When informed they were no longer available, his face dropped. 'They were my favourite thing about Fortnum's. The perfect snack.' And they are, hand-held, and covered with the very thinnest level of savoury, HP-spiked brown sauce glaze. Best eaten cold.

Serves 2

a 6-bone rack of lamb
1 tablespoon vegetable oil
80g redcurrant jelly
25g unsalted butter
1 tablespoon HP sauce
2 tablespoons chopped mint, plus extra to garnish
salt and freshly ground black pepper

Trim some of the fat off the lamb rack and scrape any flesh from the bones.

Heat the oil in an ovenproof frying pan. Season the lamb on both sides. When the oil is hot, add the lamb fat side down and brown over a medium heat. Turn to brown on the other side, then transfer to an oven heated to 180°C/Gas Mark 4 and roast for 12–15 minutes; this should give meat that is pink in the centre. Remove from the oven and leave to rest in a warm place while you make the glaze.

Melt the redcurrant jelly gently in a small saucepan with the butter and then add the HP sauce. Stir until smooth, then mix in a spoonful of the fat from the pan in which the lamb was cooked; this will give it extra flavour. Stir in the chopped mint. Leave it to cool.

Carve the lamb into 6, cutting down between the bones. Divide between 2 serving plates and spoon the glaze on top, sprinkling with a little extra mint if you like. Chill before serving.

Lamb Chops with Tomato and Mint Salsa

This is a wonderful summer dish, where the gentle bleat of lamb chops is accentuated by a sharp tomato salsa. Do make sure to render the fat as you're cooking the cutlets. It gives them a crunchy char and is almost the best bit. And although peeling the tomatoes may seem like a bore, it takes mere moments and saves those irritating rolls of skin being stuck between your teeth.

Serves 2

6 lamb cutlets
a little olive oil
salt and freshly ground black pepper

For the tomato and mint salsa
4 plum tomatoes
2 shallots
1 tablespoon white wine vinegar, preferably Chardonnay vinegar
2 tablespoons olive oil
8 mint leaves, very finely chopped
10 flat-leaf parsley leaves, very finely chopped

First make the salsa. Score the end of each tomato with a sharp knife (this makes it easier to remove the skin). Put the tomatoes in a bowl of boiling water and leave for about 20 seconds, then drain and place in cold water. Drain again and peel off the skins. Cut the tomatoes into quarters and scoop out and discard the seeds. Cut the flesh into neat 5mm dice.

Dice the shallots as finely as you can and transfer to a bowl. Sprinkle over the vinegar and a pinch of salt and mix well. Add the tomatoes, oil and herbs, toss lightly together, then taste and adjust the seasoning.

Rub the cutlets with a little olive oil and season with salt and pepper. Heat a large, heavy-based frying pan and add the cutlets. Leave until they are golden underneath, then turn and cook the other side. When they are cooked to your liking, remove from the heat and leave to rest for 5 minutes. Serve with the tomato and mint salsa.

Twice-baked Cheddar Cheese Soufflés with Piccalilli

Do not fear the soufflé, especially if it's twice-baked, a technique that takes any real worry out of the process. And once you've mastered the technique, it's yours for life. The key is best-quality Cheddar. At Fortnum's they use Barber's. Avoid those sweaty, pale, pre-packed blocks like the plague.

Serves 6

35g unsalted butter, plus 30g very soft butter for greasing
35g Parmesan cheese, grated
35g plain flour
235ml whole milk
170g mature farmhouse Cheddar Cheese, grated
Worcestershire sauce, Tabasco sauce and English mustard, to taste
3 medium egg yolks
4 medium egg whites
1 teaspoon cornflour
salt and freshly ground white pepper

To serve
180ml double cream
1 quantity of Piccalilli (see page 260)

Grease six 120ml ramekins (or you could use foil baking cups) with the soft butter, using a pastry brush to apply it evenly. Coat the inside of each mould with the grated Parmesan, rotating the mould in your hand to ensure it is evenly coated and tipping out the excess into the next mould. Set them aside.

Melt the butter in a small pan and stir in the flour to form a roux. Cook gently for a minute or so, then gradually stir in the milk. Bring to the boil to make a very thick béchamel. Cook for 10 minutes, stirring frequently to prevent the mixture catching on the base of the pan, then add the Cheddar cheese. Take off the heat and stir until the cheese is melted and the mixture is smooth. Season to taste with Worcestershire sauce, Tabasco, mustard, and salt and pepper; it needs to be very well seasoned because the flavour will mellow when you add the egg whites. Transfer the mixture to a large bowl and let it cool down a little, then beat in the egg yolks one at a time.

Put the egg whites into a large bowl and whisk until they form soft peaks, beating in the cornflour towards the end. Roughly mix a quarter of the egg whites into the cheese mixture to loosen it, then fold in the rest with a large metal spoon, keeping as much air in the mixture as possible.

Divide the mixture between the prepared ramekins, then place them in a large roasting tin and pour enough hot water into the tin to come about halfway up the sides of the ramekins. Transfer to an oven heated to 180°C/Gas Mark 4 and bake for 18 minutes, until the soufflés are well risen but still have a slight wobble in the centre.

Remove the ramekins from the roasting tin and leave to stand for about 5 minutes. Run a knife around

the edge of each one and turn them out into a small shallow gratin dish. Pour 2 tablespoons of the double cream over each one (you can leave them for an hour or so before finishing and they will be fine).

When you are ready to serve, place the soufflés in the oven at 180°C/Gas Mark 4. Cook for about 10 minutes, until they are heated through and have coloured a little on top. Serve immediately, with a spoonful of piccalilli.

Pork Escalopes Cordon Bleu

Ah, Cordon Bleu. Once the wide blue ribbon, upon which hung the Cross of the Holy Spirit medal, worn by the most noble knights of L'Ordre des Chevaliers du Saint-Esprit. They were famed, one story goes, for throwing dinners, 'cordons bleu', of unrivalled excellence. And extravagance too. Come the Revolution, though, and all that aristocratic excess was cut short. But the name stuck, and became synonymous with gastronomic greatness.

There's another tale (as ever in classic recipes, the origins are often as murky as unclarified stock), which draws the connection between blue silk sashes and the blue ribbons of a cook's apron. And yet another, that argues that this dish, basically schnitzel with an oozing cheese centre, gets its name from the 'cordon' of sauce that surrounds it. In reality, escalopes Cordon Bleu was probably born in Switzerland sometime in the 1940s. But whatever tale you choose to believe, there's little doubt that it's an old-school belter. Burnished breadcrumbs, oozing Gruyère, succulent pork. And a cheeky slice of ham too.

Serves 2

2 pork escalopes, weighing about 120g each
100g Gruyère cheese, sliced
2 slices of ham
30g plain flour
1 egg, lightly beaten
50g white breadcrumbs
2 tablespoons vegetable oil
salt and freshly ground black pepper
watercress, to garnish

For the sauce
40g unsalted butter
lemon juice
2 tablespoons chopped parsley
50ml reduced chicken stock

Place each pork escalope between 2 pieces of cling film and beat them flat with a meat mallet or the base of a small pan (you could ask your butcher to do this for you). Season the escalopes, put the cheese and ham on top of them and roll them up tightly. Chill for 20 minutes.

Put the flour in a shallow bowl, the egg in another and the breadcrumbs in a third. Coat each escalope first in the flour, then in the beaten egg and finally in the breadcrumbs, pressing them on lightly to make sure they stay in place.

Heat the vegetable oil in an ovenproof frying pan, add the escalopes and fry until golden brown all over. Transfer to an oven heated to 180°C/Gas Mark 4 and cook for 8 minutes.

In a separate frying pan, heat the butter until it is foamy and turns golden brown. Add a good squeeze of lemon juice to stop the butter colouring too much, then remove from the heat and stir in the chopped parsley. Finish with the chicken stock.

Place each escalope on a serving plate, pour over the sauce and garnish with watercress.

Coffee

At Fortnum's, they grind your coffee beans to order. Of course they do. Because all those delectable oils, the things that scent your cup and please the palate, start to dissipate within moments of being exposed to air. So you want the least possible time between grind and brew. The true aficionados come to the store and buy their beans whole. Then do all the work at home. Either way, to taste the greatest expression of the subtleties and idiosyncrasies of any roasted coffee bean, you've got to go fresh.

The coffee bean, though, is not actually a bean, rather a seed of the coffea plant. Which is native to tropical Africa. Yet once proof of its miraculous powers spread, so too did the plant, and it's now cultivated in over 70 countries. The earliest mention is found in the writings of Rhazes, an Arabian physician, some time in the tenth century. And as ever, there are bushels of fantastical tales. Like one involving a goat-herder who, having watched his beasts eat the red berries and then go cock-a-bloody-loop, decides to try a few himself. The high is so thrilling that he runs to the nearby monastery, eyes wide and heart beating fast. The monks, of course, have little time for such unholy stimulation. So throw the beans onto the fire. Attracting more monks, seduced by the smell. The now roasted beans are pulled from the embers, ground up and added to water. And hey presto, the cup of coffee is born. Apocryphal, perhaps, but not without charm.

Anyway, the berries were eaten first, whole or mixed with animal fat, to produce a protein-rich mouthful. And later, booze was made from the fermented pulp. Legend has it that it travelled from medieval Ethiopia to Arabia, where the world domination really began. But it was only at the start of the thirteenth century that the beans started being roasted, ground and mixed with water. In the Yemen, the brew was called *Qahwah* (derived from *qaha*, 'to lack hunger'), which was also a rather lyrical name for wine. This super-brew allowed the devoted to pray deep into the night, and Dervish and Muslim pilgrims helped spread the drink, in the fifteenth and sixteenth centuries, through the East (near and middle) as well as North Africa.

So when did the coffee seed hit Europe? Scholars can (and do) spend hours arguing the finer points, but most seem to agree that it first landed in Italy, probably Venice, at some point in the sixteenth century. The original British coffee house was opened in Oxford in 1650 by Jacob, a Turkish Jew. And one of the Fortnum's family was actually coffee-man to the university in the mid-eighteenth century. Despite its rapid acceptance, though, coffee was often seen as a subversive brew. Thriving coffee shops meant empty churches and mosques. 'Satan's latest trap to catch Christian souls,' as the Vatican so subtly put it. By the middle of the eighteenth century, coffee had travelled to the New World, as well as South India. The global caffeine addiction had begun.

Fortnum & Mason have had a long relationship with coffee, and were one of the first roasters in London. And their buyers continue to crisscross the globe, from Costa Rica to Ethiopia, Guatemala and Colombia to Tanzania and Kenya, in search of coffee nirvana.

There are two types of bean – Robusta, strong, hardy and not madly subtle. It makes up 40 per cent of sales. The other, more delicate, and far less easy to grow, is the Arabica bean. Making it more desirable, but more expensive too. And all Fortnum's coffee is made from Arabica beans. Once the coffee cherry is ripe, it's harvested (by hand, if possible, which means only the very ripest are chosen). The most traditional dry method involves sun-drying the ripe red cherries. They are constantly turned, to avoid spoiling, then covered at night (and during rain) to keep them dry. This process can go on for many weeks, until the desired moisture content (around 11 per cent) is reached. More recently, machines have been used to dry the beans too. Then they're sorted, graded and exported in 60–70kg jute sacks.

Unlike tea, coffee is pretty much always roasted in the country of import, rather than export, to ensure the punter gets the best possible taste. Roasts range from cinnamon (very light) to city charcoal (dark and dirty). The Fortnum's blends are mostly medium roast. And as with wine and tea, terroir is everything, with each estate, area and country giving their own distinct character to the beans.

And it's here among the Single Estates, where the truest expression of coffee can be found. The rounded, gentle, complex and fragrant charms of Jamaican Blue Mountain, from Clifton Mount Estate; the rather more rich and aromatic tang of Colombia Cascada, from Finca La Cascada, high up in the mountainous Antioquia region; elegant, naturally processed Panama Esmerelda Special (auctioned only once per year, in nano lots), with its jasmine aroma and melon and papaya tasting notes; Old Brown Java Bondowoso, dark and suited to after-dinner drinking, rich with creamy, bittersweet chocolate allure. Or the juicy, vibrant and complex charms of Kenya Ngandu smallholder lots. The range at Fortnum's is thrillingly varied.

The Blends are a mix. Obviously. Steady, consistent, reliable. Breakfast is easy, balanced, full-flavoured and fruity, a cup to set up the day, with beans from Guatemala, Costa Rica and Colombia. Cabinet, originally created for Gladstone's Cabinet (much needed to stay awake as the great man droned on), is rich and zesty, made with beans from Panama, Guatemala and Bolivia. Club Blend sees a darker roast, using beans from India, Sumatra and Brazil. Bold and malty, it's smooth and full-bodied too. The Queen's Blend, with fresh fruit and caramel notes, is bright, sweet and softly exuberant. While After Dinner Viennese Blend is strong and versatile, perfect for after dinner sipping.

Then there's the actual brewing. The traditional European taste is for heavily roasted beans, bitter, strong and bold coffee. Think Neapolitan espresso, or a big Parisian *café au lait*. But in Australia and New Zealand, things are more subtle and blended. They take it very seriously over there.

Espresso is a fine grind, and water is pushed through it at high pressure, up to 9 bar in the most expensive Fortnum's machines. They typically use a blend, as it's easy to keep a consistent flavour profile throughout the year. Automatic drip-brewing (not to be confused with the old-style percolators – any remaining examples of these brutally basic brewers should be binned) can give wonderful results as long as the coffee is fresh, the water filtered and the machine clean. The true coffee nuts love the likes of V60 or Chemex manual filter devices, which coax out even more flavour.

Oh, and don't store your coffee in the fridge – it tends to sweat and start brewing. Just keep it away from light and air. Okay, so proper coffee is still about the meeting of ground bean and hot water. But forget about that freeze-dried rubbish. And come to where the flavour really is.

Sides

‘Every expedient known to science is employed each winter to make our fruit and vegetables the earliest’

Artichokes with Sage and Parmesan

Both kinds, globe and Jerusalem, scattered with Parmesan. A little whisper of Italy in this most British of stores.

Serves 4

1 lemon, cut in half
4 globe artichokes
4 medium Jerusalem artichokes
50ml olive oil
100ml white wine
1 tablespoon chopped sage
30g Parmesan cheese, freshly grated
salt and freshly ground black pepper

Squeeze one of the lemon halves into a bowl of water, adding the squeezed-out lemon half to the water too. Cut the stalks off the globe artichokes and strip off all the dark green leaves. Slice off the top of each artichoke and then use a small, sharp knife to pare off the leaves round the base of the heart, trimming it until all the tough bits have been removed. Scoop out the fuzzy choke with a teaspoon and discard. Cut each artichoke heart into quarters, adding them to the bowl of acidulated water as you go. If the artichokes start to discolour as you prepare them, rub them with the other lemon half.

Peel the Jerusalem artichokes and cut them in half, adding them to the bowl of water as they are done to prevent discoloration.

Heat the olive oil in a shallow pan that is large enough to hold all the artichokes in a single layer. Drain the artichokes well, add them to the pan and cook gently until coloured all over. Pour in the white wine and braise in the oven at 170°C/Gas Mark 3 until the artichokes are tender (if some pieces are done before others, remove them from the pan and set aside).

Once they are all cooked, remove the pan from the heat and leave for about 5 minutes to cool a little. Stir in the sage and season to taste.

Transfer the artichokes to a serving plate, then spoon a little of the cooking juices over them. Sprinkle with the Parmesan and serve straight away.

Celeriac Dauphinoise

This simply adds earthy celeriac to equally earthy potato. The key is to slice the roots on a mandoline, as thin as you dare. Crushed garlic is infused with cream, poured over and allowed to bubble and brown. Good enough to eat on its own.

Serves 4

500g large King Edward potatoes
1 celeriac
1 small onion
100ml whole milk
200ml double cream
1 garlic clove, crushed to a paste with a pinch of salt
a pinch of freshly grated nutmeg
leaves from a sprig of thyme
a little butter, for greasing
salt and freshly ground black pepper
chopped parsley, to garnish

Peel the potatoes and celeriac, then slice them on a mandoline to about 1mm thick; if you don't have a mandoline, slice them by hand as thinly as you can.

Peel and halve the onion and slice it as thinly as possible into half-moon shapes.

Put the milk, cream, garlic, nutmeg and thyme into a saucepan and bring to the boil.

Grease a shallow ovenproof dish and arrange the potatoes, celeriac and onion in it in layers, seasoning each layer and pouring over a little of the milk and cream mixture as you go. Cover with foil and place in an oven heated to 180°C/Gas Mark 4. Bake for 1–1½ hours, until the vegetables are tender when a knife is inserted in the centre. Remove the foil halfway through cooking to allow the top to crisp up and colour. Sprinkle with chopped parsley before serving.

Braised Baby Gems with Orange and Star Anise

Don't worry about cooking lettuce; Little Gems have the body to take it. A great side dish to serve with fish. Modern, and rather refreshing too.

Serves 4

4 baby Little Gem lettuces
2 tablespoons olive oil
200ml freshly squeezed orange juice
1 star anise
30g unsalted butter, diced
salt and freshly ground black pepper

Trim the brown ends off the lettuces and cut them lengthwise in half. Give them a quick wash in cold water and place on a cloth to dry.

Heat the olive oil in an ovenproof frying pan into which the lettuce halves will fit in a single layer. Lightly season the lettuce and place in the pan, cut side down. Leave for a minute or so, until golden brown. Flip them over and cook for 30 seconds, then add the orange juice and star anise. When the orange juice starts to simmer, transfer the pan to an oven heated to 180°C/Gas Mark 4. Cook for about 6 minutes, until the lettuce is tender but still has a slight crunch.

Remove from the oven and transfer the lettuce halves to a dish. Strain the orange juice through a fine sieve into a small pan and simmer until reduced by about half. Whisk in the butter a couple of cubes at a time. Season to taste, pour the sauce over the lettuces and serve straight away.

Petits Pois à la Française

Onions, chicken stock, Little Gem lettuce and petits pois, a dish that turns a fine ingredient into an even finer dish. Use frozen, of course. Unless you're cooking in mid-summer, when fresh are at their sweetest.

Serves 4

50g unsalted butter
1 small onion, thinly sliced
100g bacon lardons
200g fresh or frozen petits pois
50ml white wine
80ml chicken or vegetable stock
1 small Little Gem lettuce, thinly sliced
salt and freshly ground black pepper

Melt the butter in a saucepan, add the onion and bacon and cook gently for about 5 minutes, until the onion is softened but not coloured. Add the petits pois and white wine and simmer for 2 minutes.

Pour in the stock and cook for 2 minutes longer, then add the lettuce. Cook, stirring constantly, until the lettuce is wilted and tender. Season with salt and pepper to taste.

Glazed Parsnips with Honey

The key is good honey and lashings of butter, to get that rich, caramel-like glaze. This is sweet, no denying that. A little goes a long way. Parsley freshens it up at the end.

Serves 4

800g parsnips
2 tablespoons vegetable oil
30g unsalted butter
20g honey
10g light soft brown sugar
3 tablespoons chopped flat-leaf parsley
salt and freshly ground black pepper

Peel the parsnips and cut them into slices 5cm thick. Cut these into rough batons, removing some of the core. Put into a pan of boiling salted water and simmer for 2–3 minutes, then drain well.

Put the parsnips on a baking tray with the vegetable oil and mix together. Place in an oven heated to 190°C/Gas Mark 5 and cook for 25–30 minutes, until they are tender and golden. Remove from the oven and set aside.

Heat the butter, honey and brown sugar in a large frying pan until they form a syrup. Add the parsnips and some salt and pepper and cook until they are lightly glazed with the honey mixture. Sprinkle with the chopped parsley.

A Note on the Illustrations

Colonel Charles Wyld may have been a veteran of both Boer and First World Wars. But he was no ordinary soldier. Not only did he have strong links, particularly via his niece, with the more progressive part of the art world, in an age where army and the avant-garde were not exactly natural bedfellows, but also he was perhaps the most revolutionary Managing Director in Fortnum & Mason history.

Wyld joined the firm in 1905, at a time when it had barely changed since early Victorian days. Employing a mere 35 men, it was a grocer with a thriving business in wines, spirits, cigars and external catering. Wyld had ambitious plans to expand the business, but these were put on hold in 1914, with the outbreak of the First World War. He was posted as second-in-command to the Rifle Depot of the 16th (Service) Battalion of the King's Royal Rifle Corps, swiftly scaling the ranks until he reached Lieutenant-Colonel. On his return, though, he began to buy up the leases of adjoining properties and by 1931 the esteemed royal grocer had become the revered royal department store.

It still catered, to an upmarket crowd, with the likes of Joyce Wethered, the world-class lady golf champion, employed in the sports department. But it was his partnership with Hugh Stuart Menzies – who not only headed up the firm's Invalid department, but also ran the Stuart Advertising Agency, the holder of the Fortnum's advertising account – which produced the Commentaries, the beautifully written and illustrated direct marketing booklets of the 1930s from which so many of this book's illustrations are taken.

'Go ahead, work out the idea and we'll try it,' said the visionary Wyld to the equally brilliant Menzies. 'I visualised little booklets,' the latter said of the Commentaries, 'sent to a carefully chosen mailing list; booklets as readable as something bought at a bookstall or drawn from the library. Every preconceived notion of a trade catalogue was to be violated. Space was to be sacrificed to pure fun in every direction...' He certainly succeeded. To revel in his honeyed words is bliss. Anchovy wafers, 'as limpid as the Biscay rollers at Biarritz.' Chutneys 'that move us to such a passion of enthusiasm we can hardly bear to speak of them in cold print.' And fruit, 'in bottles, and divorced from the distractions of the world. Our cherries meditate in kind old brandy.'

And the envelope was every bit as important as the catalogue. 'An unsealed envelope bearing a halfpenny stamp is usually thrown away unopened,' Menzies went on. 'I evolved the idea of using open envelopes with a halfpenny stamp, and putting a little picture and caption on the outside, so inexplicable that people looked inside to find out what it was all about.'

Menzies' prose sparkled. But the illustrations were every bit its equal. Indeed, Menzies himself, a man of manifold talents, drew as well as wrote. W. M. Hendy, another artist and cartoonist for *Punch*, was the main illustrator in the 20s and 30s and even Edward McKnight Kauffer and Cedric Morris contributed a few sketches. But it was Edward Bawden's work that was the most famous of all, at once witty, vivid and visually striking. Especially of cats. Lots and lots of cats. He first worked for the store in 1932. And although the Second World War put an end to extravagant advertising (with rationing in full force, it was hardly the time to flog wittily-drawn luxuries), the relationship was rekindled in 1955, when rationing finally ended.

Bawden was a great artist, and is now becoming increasingly revered. With good reason. A painter, printer, illustrator and graphic designer (his work with cookery writer Ambrose Heath was joyously brilliant), he even turned his hand to iron garden furniture. A jack-of-all-trades, and a master of many, his work was never raw or tortured, an expression of soul-baring angst in the manner of Van Gogh. No, he always insisted his art was about good design. As you can see by his wonderful illustrations in this book. Wyld and Menzies could sure spot talent.

So, yes, these Commentaries were catalogues. But catalogues clad in the most elegant and exquisite finery, in true Fortnum & Mason style. And they still resound to this day – words that shimmer with wit, vim and verve, illustrations that delight and beguile. The Commentaries are timeless. Colonel Wyld would be proud.

EIIR
GEORGE VI 1936 - 1952
EDWARD VIII 1936
WILLIAM IV 1830 1837
QUEEN VICTORIA 1837-1901
EDWARD VII 1901 1910
GEORGE V 1910 - 1936
GEORGE IV 1820 - 1830
GEORGE III 1760 - 1820
This is
the twelfth reign
in which we have
been privileged
to serve
GEORGE II 1727 - 1760
GEORGE I 1714 - 1727
QUEEN ANNE 1702-1714

Pommes à la Parisienne

An old-fashioned dish that is well worth reviving. Basically really good fried potato. Use the leftover potato bits in a soup.

Serves 4

1kg red-skinned potatoes
100ml olive oil
130g unsalted butter
leaves from 6 sprigs of thyme
2 garlic cloves, peeled and lightly crushed with the back of a knife
salt and freshly ground black pepper

Peel the potatoes and then use a melon baller (also known as a Parisienne scoop) to scoop out balls of potato into a large bowl of cold water. Try to keep them as round as possible.

Heat the olive oil in a heavy-based frying pan that is large enough to hold the potatoes in a single layer. Drain the potato balls and dry them thoroughly with kitchen paper – this is important, as otherwise they will cause the oil to spit. When the oil is almost smoking, add the potatoes and fry until golden all over. Place in the oven at 180°C/Gas Mark 4 for 15–18 minutes, or until cooked, and then drain in a colander.

In a pan melt the butter, add the thyme and garlic and cook for 2 minutes. Add the potatoes to the pan, stir into the hot butter, add some salt and pepper. Cook for another 5 minutes or so, keeping the potatoes moving in the pan, until the potatoes are tender and a good golden brown colour.

Remove from the pan with a slotted spoon and drain on kitchen paper. Season with a little more salt, and serve straight away.

Creamed Leeks with Crisp Bacon

Soft leeks, crisp bacon. Another side that could happily be devoured on its tod.

Serves 4

500g leeks (trimmed weight)
40g unsalted butter
100ml white wine
120ml double cream
1 tablespoon thyme leaves
200g streaky bacon, cut into small strips
1 tablespoon vegetable oil
salt and freshly ground black pepper

Cut the leeks lengthwise in half and then into 4cm strips. Melt the butter in a saucepan, add the leeks and some salt and pepper and cook until soft but not coloured. Add the white wine and simmer until reduced by about three-quarters. Finally, add the double cream and the thyme and simmer for 2–3 minutes, until the cream is coating the leeks lightly. Taste and adjust the seasoning.

Fry the bacon in the vegetable oil until crisp. Drain thoroughly. To serve, place the hot creamed leeks in a small dish and sprinkle with the bacon.

Puddings

'In the grand manner are they made'

Raspberry Trifle

There's nothing silly about a trifle. Especially when all of those biscuits are soaked in raspberry liqueur. This is a simple summer trifle with no jelly. Don't panic at the length of the recipe as it's just an assembly job. All you have to do is make the custard. Serve it in the deepest bowl you can find.

Serves 8

about 4 tablespoons raspberry jam
1 packet of ladyfinger biscuits
120ml raspberry liqueur, such as Chambord
500g raspberries
400ml double cream, lightly whipped
a small handful of flaked almonds, lightly toasted

For the custard
500ml whole milk
1 vanilla pod
4 egg yolks
70g caster sugar
1½ tablespoons cornflour

First make the custard. Pour the milk into a pan. Slit the vanilla pod open lengthwise, scrape out the seeds and add the seeds and pod to the milk. Bring to boiling point. Meanwhile, beat the egg yolks, sugar and cornflour together in a bowl. Gradually pour the hot milk on to the egg yolk mixture, stirring constantly with a wooden spoon. Pour the mixture back into the pan and cook, stirring, over a low to medium heat until thickened. Strain the custard into a bowl and cover the surface with cling film to prevent a skin forming. Leave to cool, then chill.

To assemble the trifle, spread the jam over the base of a deep, 20cm glass dish. Cover the jam with half the ladyfinger biscuits and sprinkle with half the raspberry liqueur. Scatter half the raspberries on top and cover with half the custard. Spoon or pipe half the whipped cream over. Repeat these layers (minus the jam), then sprinkle the toasted almonds on top. Chill until ready to serve.

Steamed Marmalade Pudding with Vanilla Custard

The art of the pudding is an elegant one – comfort without stodge, and a feeling of lightness in amongst all that sponge. Do be generous with the marmalade. If you want to make a quick sauce, simply heat a few tablespoons of marmalade with a spoonful of orange juice and a dash of whisky or brandy, then pour over the pudding.

Serves 4–6

175g marmalade
100g softened unsalted butter
100g caster sugar
grated zest of 1 orange
2 large eggs, lightly beaten
160g plain flour
10g baking powder
40ml milk

For the vanilla custard
250ml whole milk
250ml double cream
1 vanilla pod
6 egg yolks
115g caster sugar
10g cornflour

Grease a 900ml pudding basin and line the base with a circle of baking parchment. Spoon the marmalade into the basin.

Beat the butter, sugar and orange zest together until light and fluffy. Beat in the eggs a little at a time, then sift in the flour and baking powder. Fold them in with a large metal spoon. Finally, fold in the milk.

Transfer the mixture to the pudding basin. Cover the top of the basin with a piece of baking parchment with a pleat down the centre, then with a piece of pleated foil. Tie them securely under the rim of the basin with string. Place the basin in a metal steamer set over a pan of simmering water and steam for 1½ hours, topping up the water with more boiling water as necessary.

Meanwhile, make the vanilla custard. Put the milk and cream into a pan. Slit the vanilla pod open lengthwise and scrape out the seeds, then add both pod and seeds to the pan and bring to a simmer. Beat the egg yolks, sugar and cornflour together in a bowl. Gradually pour in half the hot milk mixture, beating constantly. Return this mixture to the pan and cook over a gentle heat, stirring all the time, until it starts to thicken. Remove from the heat immediately and strain through a fine sieve into a bowl. Leave to cool, stirring occasionally to prevent a skin forming.

Remove the foil and baking parchment from the pudding, run a knife around the side of the bowl and turn the pudding out on to a plate. Serve immediately, with the custard on the side.

Rose Petal Pudding

A rosewater-flavoured summer pudding, decorated with rose petals. If the months are more autumnal, swap the strawberries for blackberries and currants.

Serves 6

750g seasonal berries
110g caster sugar
10g cornflour
½ vanilla pod
grated zest of ½ orange
1–2 tablespoons rosewater
7–8 slices from a large white loaf, crusts removed
a few fresh, unsprayed rose petals, to decorate

Put the berries into a saucepan with the sugar, cornflour, vanilla pod and orange zest and mix well. Heat gently, then bring to a simmer and cook for 1–2 minutes. Remove from the heat and add rosewater to taste. Set 3–4 tablespoons of the compote aside, then drain the rest of the fruit, reserving the liquid.

Line a 1-litre basin with cling film and allow enough overhang to cover the whole pudding once the basin is filled. Cut a circle out of one slice of bread to fit the bottom of the basin. Dip it in the juices from the compote and put it into the basin. Cut the remaining slices in half on the diagonal and use them to line the sides of the basin, dipping each one in juice as you go. Be sure to overlap them slightly as you fit them round the edge of the basin, so there are no gaps.

Fill the bread-lined basin with the berries, removing the vanilla pod. Cut a final piece of bread to fit the top and dip it in the juice. Pour the remaining juice into the basin and top with the bread. Cover with the cling film then with a plate that just fits inside the basin, then put a weight on top – a tin of beans will do nicely. Leave in the fridge overnight.

To serve, run a knife around the edge of the pudding, turn it out on to a plate and pour over the reserved compote. Scatter a few rose petals over the top. It's good served with plenty of thick cream.

Jam

Jam tomorrow, jam yesterday, but never jam today – in life, this mantra can be all too true. But at Fortnum's, it's jam every day. Over thirty varieties, glittering prettily in the Jam Temple, a Food Hall wall devoted to the sweet, sticky and seductive. Preserves have been at the heart of Fortnum & Mason since the start in 1707, when they sold sugar along with fresh oranges, lemons and tangerines so that the kitchens of the great houses could make their own. A method, directly descended from marmalade-making, of preserving that taste of summer for the long, dark winter months ahead.

At this point, we must raise a sticky spoon to Nicolas Appert, the Frenchman who, in 1809, pioneered the bottling and tinning of jams. It changed the way we ate. Or the way we preserved, at the very least. Fortnum's relished this new technology, and began making their own preserves, in house, with fruit from Kent and the Vale of Evesham. Catering for an ever-expanding middle class, with only the most basic of servant support, the jams were tinned and had very high sugar levels. But they were ideal for the export market, and for those expats nostalgic for a taste of home. Shortly after the start of World War II, sugar had become as rare as plovers' eggs, and was brutally rationed. 'What do we want with eggs and ham/When we've got plum and apple jam?' they cried in the musical *Oh! What a Lovely War*. What indeed?

But sugar was so rare that there was barely a mention of jams and preserves in the catalogues between 1940 and 1952. Jam tinned and bulked out with apples, as well as cheap fruit such as pears and plums, was simply called 'Mixed Jam'. The war years saw the likes of Marrow Ginger Preserve come to the fore. Sheer necessity. Why else would you eat a marrow? Sweetening agents like oranges, raisins and even chestnuts were used in place of the elusive sugar. But quality and consistency was all, and standards never dropped.

Nothing has changed. Every single product has to pass the lips of the chief buyer. If it's too sweet, or sticky, or lumpy, or smooth, it gets sent back. All Fortnum's jams are still made the old-fashioned way, in small, bubbling pans. They're stirred by hand too, unlike commercially made jams, which are made in vast, uniform and standardised batches, with little need for the human touch. And detail is everything – from the type of sugar used (demerara for light preserves, muscovado for a deeper, richer, heft) to the type of strawberry (in the Strawberry Preserve, say, there's a mix of Cambridge Favourite and Tioga, to get that perfect spreading texture), to added booze (Champagne and Strawberry Jam is topped with real, house-brand Fortnum's Champagne; using inferior industrial alcohol would ride roughshod over any delicate nuances). As for the Woodland Strawberry . . . it's made with only wild Scottish berries. The king of jams, perhaps, but just one of many.

Another classic is the Rose Petal Jelly. Not any old petals, rather ones grown in a small paddock near Henley. By a lady who once worked in the Electrical Department. If there's rain, the petals cannot be harvested, as the scent is subdued. Nope, they can only be picked at night, when the sun has been shining all day, to ensure that perfect bouquet. They're relaxed overnight, before being made into jelly the next day. Lots of effort, but well worth the hassle. Because at Fortnum's, jam is never a trifling matter.

Rice Pudding with Strawberry Jam

We might remember it in its rather sullen school-dining-hall incarnation. But made properly, rice pudding is the quintessence of comfort food. It's made on the stove, not in the oven, meaning no skin. Which is good or bad, depending on your view. Strawberry jam is the classic accompaniment.

Serves 4–6

80g pudding rice
600ml whole milk
1 vanilla pod
50g caster sugar
25g unsalted butter
freshly grated nutmeg
good-quality strawberry jam, to serve

Put the pudding rice into a large, heavy-based saucepan with the milk. Slit the vanilla pod open lengthwise, scrape out the seeds, and add the seeds and the pod to the pan. Bring to the boil and simmer very gently for 30–40 minutes, until the rice is tender and most of the liquid has been absorbed. Stir frequently, particularly towards the end of cooking.

Remove the vanilla pod, stir in the sugar and butter and cook for a minute or so longer. Grate over nutmeg to taste. Divide between serving bowls, topping each portion with a spoonful of jam.

Mark Hix's Earlgazey Pond Pudding

Stephen Fry named this, at a particularly fine Fortnum's boardroom lunch. Mark Hix, who was behind the revival of Stargazey Pie (an old West-Country dish), created the recipe, replacing the lemon in Sussex Pond Pudding with the more exotic bergamot, the fruit that scents Earl Grey. So Fry decided that Earlgazey Pond Pudding was a more suitable name. And it stuck. If bergamots are out of season, use a whole lemon instead.

Serves 4–6

250g self-raising flour
125g shredded beef suet or vegetable suet
150ml milk
300g softened unsalted butter, plus extra for the basin
200g light soft brown sugar
1 large bergamot or lemon

Mix the flour and suet together in a bowl. Gradually add the milk, stirring to make a dough. It should be soft but not sticky. Roll it out on a lightly floured work surface into a circle large enough to line a 1.5-litre pudding basin. Cut a quarter out of the circle, so that you can make a cone shape with the dough to fit more easily into the pudding basin, leaving leftover dough for the lid. Put this slice of dough aside. Grease the pudding basin well and drop the pastry into it, flattening it at the bottom and joining up the edges where the slice was taken out.

Mix the butter and sugar together and put them into the lined basin. Prick the bergamot or lemon all over as much as you can with a roasting fork or skewer so that the juices can escape, then push it into the butter mixture. Re-roll the reserved piece of pastry into a circle large enough to fit the top of the pudding basin. Lay it over the filling and press the edges of the dough together so that the filling is sealed in.

Take a piece of foil big enough to fit over the basin and with at least an extra 5cm all round. Make a pleat down the middle of the foil, place it over the top of the basin and tie in place with string under the rim of the basin, or tie like a parcel with a string handle so it can be lifted in and out of the saucepan. Bring a large pan half-filled with water to the boil and lower in the pudding. Cover and leave to simmer for 4 hours. Don't let the water stop boiling and, if the level drops, lift up the basin and top up the pan with more boiling water.

To serve, lift out the basin, remove the foil and run a small sharp knife around the side to loosen the pudding. (It can be kept hot for another hour or so until it is needed.) Put a deep dish over the basin and quickly turn the whole thing upside down.

Panettone Bread and Butter Pudding

Panettone replaces bread in this ultra-luxe take on the British classic. Gilded nursery food with a strong Italian accent. If panettone is unavailable, use fruit loaf or tea cakes instead.

Serves 6

40g softened unsalted butter
freshly grated nutmeg
ground cinnamon
300g panettone, cut into slices about 8mm thick
1 vanilla pod
250ml double cream
250ml milk
3 eggs
1 egg yolk
125g caster sugar

Liberally grease an ovenproof dish, roughly 23cm square, with the softened butter, then dust it with a little nutmeg and cinnamon. Layer the panettone slices in the dish and set aside.

Slit the vanilla pod open lengthwise and scrape out the seeds. Put the seeds and pod into a pan with the cream and milk and bring to simmering point. Beat the eggs and extra yolk with the sugar in a bowl until well combined. Gradually pour on the hot cream mixture, stirring constantly.

Strain this custard through a sieve into a jug and pour it over the panettone, allowing it to soak up the liquid. Leave to stand for about 10 minutes. Place a piece of cardboard or a folded dishcloth on the base of a roasting tin. Place the panettone dish on top then pour enough hot water into the tin to come about halfway up the sides of the dish. Bake in an oven heated to 140°C/Gas Mark 1 for 35–40 minutes, until the pudding is browned on top and the custard is just set. Leave to stand for about 15 minutes before serving.

Honey

Honey. A taste as old as spring water, the very distillation of flowers, meadows and sunshine. Pure, concentrated nectar, it's a sweetener of tea, cake and civilisation alike, an eternal symbol of health, wealth and plenty. Spread thin on hot buttered toast, dribbled over pecorino cheese, brushed over lamb chops, swirled into ice cream or glazed over carrots, it's an ingredient as versatile as it is vibrant. And it runs thick through the history of Fortnum's.

In the eighteenth and nineteenth centuries, they sold British honeycomb alone. But as trade routes opened, so honey flowed in from across the globe, displayed in vast vessels and decanted into smaller jars at the counter: Sardinian, gathered from perilous heights, with a whisper of wild herbs; Spanish Orange Blossom, French Lavender, Hungarian Acacia; honey on the comb (the purest, rawest form of honey); even Pitcairn Island honey, made from the nectar of lata, passion flower, guava and roseapple in one of the least polluted (and most remote) places on Earth. Each with its own charms, floral notes and delectable idiosyncrasies.

Then there are the British varieties, from Salisbury Plain and Shropshire to Single Estates from Yorkshire, Essex, Wales and Wiltshire. So different from the dull, mass-market blended honeys that show little interest in provenance and individual nuance. Fortnum's even have their own hives on the roof of the store. Not any old run-of-the-mill apiary, but specially designed, eau-de-nil tinted neo-classical palaces, with pagoda-shaped roofs and entrances surrounded by a triumphal arch. The Blenheim of beehives, filled with native Buckfast Bees, feasting on the flowers of Green Park, Clarence House and Buckingham Palace. A regal mouthful indeed. Plus three more hive sites, in St Pancras, Bermondsey, and Hoxton, for that true London tang. With little farming within the M25, the end product is free of pesticides too.

In its natural state, freshly gathered from the hive, honey is runny. But some varieties, depending on where the nectar came from and the conditions in which they are kept, will crystallise and turn hard. To soften, simply put the jar into a bowl of just-boiled water and leave for 20 minutes or so.

Honeys that come from a single source of nectar, a lavender field, say, are known as monofloral or varietal, while the majority (the London honeys, for example) are multifloral. But all honey has a long shelf life. Indeed, tales abound of honey found deep in ancient Egyptian pyramids being pronounced perfect, thousands of years on. Admittedly, honey is at its finest when fresh, but it will keep for many years after that. Store at room temperature, with a top, and away from the fridge.

As to cooking, it rather depends what you're after. Light, delicate honeys such as acacia are great for mixing into cocktails or dribbling over strawberries and the mildest of cheeses. Medium-coloured honeys, with more depth and darkness, keep their character in glazes and marinades, as well as the heavier end of the cake and pudding spectrum. The darkest of all, sometimes almost pitch-black, should be handled with care, as they tend to dominate and trample over any lesser flavours. However, honey is not only one of nature's greatest ingredients but a tribute to the humble bee. In the words of Emily Dickinson, 'The pedigree of honey/Does not concern the bee;/A clover, any time, to him/Is aristocracy.'

Treacle Tart

Don't stint on the golden syrup. And Fortnum's use a little lemon and ginger to bring out all those luscious curves. Serve with clotted cream.

Serves 8

25g unsalted butter
30g demerara sugar
375g golden syrup
30g clotted cream
juice and grated zest of ½ orange
juice and grated zest of ½ lemon
150g fresh white breadcrumbs
1 apple, peeled and grated
2 teaspoons ground ginger

For the sweet pastry
150g slightly softened unsalted butter
140g caster sugar
300g '00' flour
1 egg, lightly beaten, plus 1 extra yolk, for glazing
30ml milk

Gently melt the butter in a heavy-based pan. Add the demerara sugar and stir until the sugar dissolves slightly. Stir in the golden syrup, followed by the clotted cream and the orange and lemon juice and zest. Mix until everything has combined into a smooth, warm syrup; be careful not to let it boil.

Put the breadcrumbs, grated apple and ginger into a bowl and stir to combine. Pour on the warm golden syrup mixture and mix with a plastic spatula to make sure all the dry ingredients are saturated with the syrup. Cover and leave overnight; this gives the breadcrumbs time to soak up the syrup.

To make the pastry, cream the butter and sugar together until combined, then add half the flour and mix well. Stir in the egg and milk, then add the rest of the flour. Mix until a dough is formed. Wrap in cling film and chill for about an hour before use.

Roll out half the pastry and use to line a 25cm loose-bottomed tart tin. Line with baking parchment, fill with baking beans or rice and place in an oven heated to 180°C/Gas Mark 4. Bake blind for 15 minutes, then remove the parchment and beans or rice and bake for about 5 minutes more, until very lightly coloured. Remove from the oven and leave to cool. Pour in the filling.

Roll out the remaining pastry and cut it into 1cm-wide strips. Arrange them in a lattice on top of the tart, trimming the ends and pressing them gently onto the pastry edge. Lightly beat the extra egg yolk with a pastry brush, then brush it over the lattice. Return the tart to the oven and bake at 140°C/Gas Mark 1 for about 30 minutes, until just firm to the touch. Serve warm, accompanied by clotted cream.

Pear Tatin, Vanilla Crème Fraîche

A classic French dish, the traditional apples replaced by pears and a modern, gently lactic crème fraîche.

Serves 4

300g caster sugar
100g unsalted butter
4 ripe Conference pears
400g all-butter puff pastry
(bought is fine)
flour, for dusting
½ vanilla pod
100ml crème fraîche

Put a heavy-based pan over a medium heat and add 100g of the sugar. Leave until melted, shaking the pan occasionally so it heats evenly. Add another 100g sugar and repeat, then add the final batch. When all the sugar has melted and you have a golden-brown caramel, remove the pan from the heat and stir in the butter. Carefully pour the caramel into 4 individual non-stick tart tins, filling them about a third full. Leave to cool a little.

Peel, core and slice the pears and arrange them on top of the caramel. Roll out the puff pastry on a lightly floured surface and cut out 4 discs about 1cm larger than the tart tins. Place on top of the pears, tucking the excess pastry down the sides of the tins quite firmly. Place in an oven heated to 180°C/Gas Mark 4 and cook for 30 minutes, until the pastry is golden brown.

Meanwhile, slit open the vanilla pod and scrape out the seeds. Stir them into the crème fraîche.

When the tarts are done, remove from the oven and leave to stand for 5 minutes. Then run a knife around the sides of each tart and turn out on to a serving plate. Top with a scoop of crème fraîche and serve immediately.

Ewan's Original Scottish Tablet

This tablet, or Scottish fudge, really is knock-out. It does take a good half hour of stirring, and make sure you have that ice-cold water to hand. Well worth the effort.

Makes about 60 pieces

80g salted butter
240ml whole milk
1 x 397g tin of condensed milk
900g granulated sugar

Before you start cooking, line a medium baking tin with baking parchment and fill the kitchen sink with ice-cold water – it should be deep enough to sit the pan in after cooking, without letting water in over the top of it.

Put the butter and milk into a large, heavy-based pan and place over a low heat. When the butter has melted, add the condensed milk and stir until smooth. Then add the sugar and stir with a wooden spoon over a low heat until it has completely dissolved. Keep stirring over a low heat for 30 minutes in total, making sure that the mixture doesn't boil or catch on the base of the pan. As you stir, you will see the colour change from pale cream to a richer, more golden shade.

After 30 minutes, turn up the heat and keep stirring for about another 10 minutes, until the colour darkens further and the mixture starts to pull away from the sides of the pan. You should smell a delicious sugary, almost caramel-like aroma. (Don't be tempted to touch the mixture. It is dangerously hot.) Remove the pan from the heat and immediately place it in the ice-cold water, continuing to stir the mixture energetically. When it starts to thicken, pour out the mixture into the lined baking tin. Leave to cool, then score it into pieces. Store in an airtight container.

Paris-Brest

This is a recipe that requires a whole afternoon. Basically, profiteroles that dare to dream big. Lots of choux pastry filled with hazelnuts and pastry cream. Created in 1910 to commemorate the Paris bicycle race, it's shaped like a wheel. All those calories make for good cycling fuel.

Hazelnut paste is available from some online suppliers, but you can substitute Nutella for a subtle, chocolatey taste.

Makes 6

For the choux pastry
70g plain flour
50ml whole milk
50ml water
50g unsalted butter, diced
2 medium eggs, lightly beaten
40g flaked almonds, lightly toasted
icing sugar, for dusting

For the hazelnut pastry cream
1 vanilla pod
350ml whole milk
85g caster sugar
4 large egg yolks
30g cornflour
30g unsalted butter
120g hazelnut paste

First make the choux pastry. Sift the flour on to a small sheet of baking parchment. Put the milk, water and butter in a saucepan over a medium heat. When the butter has melted and the mixture has come to the boil, immediately remove from the heat and beat in the flour with a wooden spoon. Return to the heat and cook, stirring, for 2 minutes. Leave to cool for 5–10 minutes, so it is warm rather than hot. Using a handheld electric mixer, beat in the eggs a little at a time until they are fully incorporated. The mixture should be thick and glossy and should fall from a spoon if you shake it slightly. Transfer the choux pastry to a piping bag fitted with a 1cm nozzle.

Line a baking sheet with baking parchment. Pipe 6 choux pastry rings, about 6cm in diameter, on to it, then pipe another ring on top of each one. Sprinkle with the flaked almonds. Place in an oven heated to 200°C/Gas Mark 6 and bake for 25–30 minutes, until well risen and golden brown. They should sound crisp and hollow if you tap them underneath. Remove from the oven, made a couple of small holes in the base of each one to release the steam, then transfer to a wire rack to cool.

Next make the pastry cream. Slit the vanilla pod open lengthwise and scrape out the seeds. Put the pod and seeds in a pan with the milk and bring to the boil, then remove from the heat and set aside. Beat the sugar, egg yolks and cornflour together in a large bowl. Gradually pour on the hot milk, whisking well. Pass the mixture through a fine sieve back into the pan and cook over a low to medium heat, stirring constantly, until it thickens. It might go lumpy as it starts to thicken but just keep stirring and it will become smooth again. Reduce the heat and cook gently for 2 minutes. Remove from the heat and mix in the butter and

the hazelnut paste, then transfer to a bowl. Press a sheet of cling film over the surface and leave to cool. Whisk briefly to ensure there are no lumps, then transfer to a piping bag fitted with a star nozzle.

To assemble, slice each choux ring in half with a serrated knife. Pipe the hazelnut pastry cream into the bottom half of each one and replace the top. Dust with icing sugar.

Elvas Plums

These delectable sugarplums might have inspired their very own fairy, the ruler of the Land of the Sweets in Tchaikovsky's *The Nutcracker*. And for some, they're the very essence of Christmas past and present. In fact, they were so adored that Fortnum's would take out a two-line advertisement in *The Times* each October, announcing their arrival in store. But the actual fruits are not plums, rather greengages, grown in the Upper Alentejo region of Portugal, near to the city of Elvas. They were made popular in this country by the all-powerful British port families, who brought these delicacies (originally made by nuns for the Portuguese aristocracy) back home with them in the nineteenth century. They fast became a Yuletide staple, alongside sticky dates, boar's heads and a good old-fashioned family row.

The Duke of Wellington became a connoisseur (although he wasn't a man known for the delicacy of his palate) when the British Army, under his charge, was camped near Elvas. And although the machinery has moved with the times, the candying process remains the same as it was two centuries back. These 'plums' are hand-selected in June, blanched, then steeped in vats of sugar cane syrup for two months. After that they are washed, sun-dried and packed tightly into pretty balsawood boxes. These sweet morsels, plump as a baby's cheek, inspire the most fervent of admirers. There are dozens of customers who, on the run-up to Christmas, make their annual trip to the store to stock up. But although they are very much a seasonal treat, they're available in the store all year round. They go well with port, naturally, but also with Cognac and Armagnac, as well as cheese – both hard, fruity cow's and delicate goat's. Far too good, in short, to save for Christmas alone.

F M
take pleasure
in presenting the
good things of life
for Christmas 1956

Supper

'All the world's a plate and all the dishes Fortnum & Mason's'

F&M

Supper

These days, supper is merely dinner without the pomp, a meal to eat clad in scruffy T-shirt and jeans rather than sharp three-piece suit, something simple, unpretentious but solid and satisfying. Traditionally, though, it was an altogether later repast, a genuine 'sup' for a long night on the grog. The equivalent, I suppose, of a modern late-night kebab.

Whereas the chapter on dinner is rather more formal, grown-up even, supper is all about comfort and easy succour. For me, though, these dishes are as suited to a solo telly dinner as they are to feasting with friends around the kitchen table. Okay, so Oeufs Drumkilbo and grilled bones are hardly a post-midnight Pot Noodle. But they're wasted on late-night sustenance alone.

F
M

Scotch Egg

The difference between a decent home-made Scotch egg and those garishly tanned habitués of the service-station chiller cabinet is blindingly obvious, even to the most leaden palate. The first wraps peppery, piggy pork around a just-oozing egg, and wears its burnished breadcrumbs like a negligée rather than bulletproof vest. The flavours are pronounced, but never bullish, the textures moving from gentle crunch to soft, satisfying chew. Served warm, with a pert pile of piccalilli by its side, it offers succour and satisfaction, a natural farmyard union. The mass-market version, on the other hand, is mean, turgid, over-processed and plain dull, with any idiosyncrasies long destroyed by industrial uniformity. A sorry snack, with all the charm of gout.

Yet we continue to devour these sorry hunks by the million. Why? The usual guff about ease, convenience and cost. But this is an astonishingly simple dish to make, and, even using the highest quality of ingredients, relatively economical too. Soft-boil egg, envelop in sausage meat, dip in breadcrumbs, deep-fry, eat. Okay, so that penultimate part, involving lots of searingly hot oil, might concern some. But compared to making chips, say, the Scotch egg is a cinch.

It was also said to have been invented by Fortnum & Mason, in either 1738 or 1788 – well, according to theatrical historian W. McQueen Pope, at least, who wrote in *Goodbye Piccadilly* that he had seen documents, in the store's archive, proving this beyond doubt. Those documents are long gone, destroyed by the Luftwaffe's bombs. But the Scotch egg and Fortnum & Mason have been intimately linked ever since. In 2015, the Chotch Egg, a holy alliance between Scotch and Easter egg was born. Dark-chocolate-spiked venison mince is wrapped around a soft-boiled egg, then dipped in fresh breadcrumbs and fried.

As to its name, there seems to be scant connection with Scotland. The ingredients are hardly tartan-clad, with nothing exclusively Scottish contained within. Some claim the name comes from the alternative meaning of the word Scotch, 'to cut, score or gash'. But any connection is tenuous, at best. Just like the argument that it's an English joke about the 'auld enemie', making fun of their supposed tight-fisted ways. But unlike the Scotch woodcock, which substitutes expensive game bird with anchovy essence, this is a dish that makes the humble egg mightily meaty. Anyway, enough on etymology, and back to the thing itself. Use the best sausage meat you can find, because outdoor, naturally reared pigs mean oodles more flavour. Season with a generous hand, and deep-fry until golden. For added thrills, mix a little black pudding or chilli with the pork. One taste of these home-made beauties, though, and the Scotch egg will transform from supermarket yawn to the burnished star of a hundred happy meals.

Scotch Eggs with Mango Chutney Mayo and Piccalilli

The great Fortnum's dish. Quality is everything. Sausage meat is relatively cheap, so buy free-range from the butcher. Happy pigs make for wonderful-tasting meat, and you really want to wallow in that flavour. Make sure the egg is a little undercooked too. The art is all in the ooze. Serve with piccalilli and eat with your hands.

Makes 8

650g sausage meat
½ teaspoon ground allspice
½ teaspoon dried white pepper
½ teaspoon fine salt
2 teaspoons dried oregano
1 teaspoon dried sage
1 garlic clove, crushed to a paste with a pinch of salt
1 small shallot, very finely chopped
10 medium eggs
100g plain flour
100g breadcrumbs, preferably Japanese panko crumbs
vegetable oil, for deep-frying
50g micro cress

For the piccalilli
1 litre water
125g caster sugar
250ml white wine vinegar
a few strands of saffron
¼ teaspoon curry powder
1 tablespoon turmeric
1 bay leaf
½ cauliflower, divided into small florets
1 courgette, diced
2 carrots, thinly sliced
1 yellow carrot, thinly sliced
3 tablespoons arrowroot

For the mango chutney mayo
¾ teaspoon turmeric
¾ teaspoon curry powder
200g mayonnaise
50g mango chutney
salt and freshly ground white pepper

To make the piccalilli, put the water, sugar, vinegar, saffron, curry powder, turmeric and bay leaf in a pan and bring to the boil, stirring to dissolve the sugar. Add the vegetables and simmer until just tender, then remove them from the pan with a slotted spoon.

Mix the arrowroot to a paste with a little water and stir it into the cooking liquid. Simmer for 1–2 minutes, until thickened, then remove from the heat and leave to cool. Return the vegetables to the mixture.

To make the mango chutney mayo, put the turmeric and curry powder in a small pan with enough water to make a loose paste. Cook over a low heat for a few minutes; this gets rid of the raw taste of the spices. Leave to cool. Mix the mayonnaise with the mango chutney, then gradually add the spice mixture, tasting as you go. Season to taste with salt and pepper and set aside.

Put the sausage meat in a bowl, add the spices, salt, dried herbs, garlic and shallot and mix well. To test the seasoning, take a teaspoonful of the mixture and fry it until cooked through. Taste it, then adjust the seasoning of the remaining mixture, if necessary.

Add 8 of the eggs to a large pan of gently simmering water and cook for 6 minutes. Drain and leave under cold running water until they are completely cold. Peel off the shells.

Fortnum & Mason
182
Piccadilly.

Divide the sausage meat into 8 portions, weighing them for accuracy, if you like – they should be about 80g each. Roll out each one between 2 sheets of cling film so that it is big enough to wrap round an egg. Lightly flour the eggs, then wrap each one in a piece of sausage meat, rolling it up in the cling film as you go and making sure that it is evenly covered, without any gaps. Twist the ends of the cling film tightly to help shape the eggs.

Put the remaining eggs in a shallow bowl and beat together. Put the remaining flour in another bowl and the breadcrumbs in a third. Remove the cling film, then dip the Scotch eggs first in flour, then in beaten egg and finally in the breadcrumbs, patting them on well with your hands.

Heat the oil in a deep-fat fryer or a large, deep saucepan to 170°C (if you use a saucepan, don't fill it more than a third full, or you risk it boiling over). Add the Scotch eggs to the hot oil, cooking them in batches so as not to overcrowd the pan. Fry for 7–8 minutes, until they are a deep golden brown, then drain well on kitchen paper (the sausage meat should be cooked right through, but if you find that it isn't, put the eggs in a moderate oven for 3–4 minutes to complete the cooking). Serve warm, garnished with the micro cress and accompanied by the mango mayo and piccalilli.

F
M

Chicken Scotch Eggs with Garlic and Thyme

A variation on the Scotch egg theme, this uses minced chicken instead of pork.

Makes 6

3 tablespoons olive oil
1 large onion, finely chopped
2 large garlic cloves, crushed to a purée with a pinch of salt
1 teaspoon finely chopped thyme
400g minced chicken
7 medium eggs
75g plain flour
75g breadcrumbs, preferably Japanese panko crumbs
vegetable oil, for deep-frying
salt and freshly ground black pepper

Heat the olive oil in a small pan, then add the onion and cook gently for 5 minutes. Stir in the garlic and thyme, cover and cook for about 20 minutes, until the onion is soft but not coloured. Remove from the heat and leave to cool.

Put the minced chicken into a bowl and mix with the cooked onion mixture, seasoning well with salt and pepper. To test the seasoning, take a teaspoonful of the mixture and fry it until cooked through. Taste it, then adjust the seasoning of the remaining mixture, if necessary.

Put 6 of the eggs into a large pan of gently simmering water and cook for 6 minutes. Drain, then leave under cold running water until they are completely cold. Peel off the shells.

Divide the chicken mixture into 6 equal portions, weighing them for accuracy, if you like. Roll out each one between 2 sheets of cling film so that it is big enough to wrap round an egg. Lightly flour the eggs, then wrap each one in a piece of the chicken mixture, rolling it up in the cling film as you go and making sure that it is evenly covered, without any gaps. Twist the ends of the cling film tightly to help shape the eggs.

Put the remaining egg into a shallow bowl and beat well. Put the remaining flour into another bowl and the breadcrumbs into a third. Remove the cling film, then dip the Scotch eggs first into the flour, then into the beaten egg and finally into the breadcrumbs, patting them on well with your hands. Chill for an hour or so, until the coating is firm.

Heat the oil to 170°C in a deep-fat fryer or a large, deep saucepan (if you use a saucepan, don't fill it more than a third full, or you risk it boiling over). Add the Scotch eggs to the hot oil, cooking them in batches so as not to overcrowd the pan. Fry for 7–8 minutes, until they are a deep golden brown, then drain well on kitchen paper. Serve warm, accompanied by a herby mayonnaise.

Oxtail Scotch Eggs

Yet another variation, this time bovine, taking slow-cooked strands of oxtail and mixing them with pork sausage meat for a one-handed meat feast.

Makes 6

150g black pudding, skinned and broken up into small pieces
100g sausage meat
2 tablespoons chopped flat-leaf parsley
7 medium eggs
75g plain flour
75g breadcrumbs, preferably Japanese panko crumbs
vegetable oil, for deep-frying
sea salt and freshly ground black pepper

For the oxtail
1kg oxtail
1 carrot, roughly chopped
1 onion, roughly chopped
1 celery stalk, roughly chopped
1 bay leaf

Put the oxtail, vegetables and bay leaf in a casserole, cover generously with water and bring to a simmer. Cover and transfer to an oven heated to 150°C/Gas Mark 2. Cook for 2–3 hours, until the meat is tender enough to pull away from the bone easily with a fork. Leave until cool enough to handle, then flake the meat off the bones and weigh it; you will need 340g.

Place the 340g of oxtail, black pudding, sausage meat, chopped parsley and some salt and pepper in a bowl and mix together well. To test the seasoning, take a teaspoonful of the mixture and fry it until cooked through. Taste it, then adjust the seasoning of the remaining mixture, if necessary.

Add 6 of the eggs to a large pan of gently simmering water and cook for 6 minutes. Drain and leave under cold running water until they are completely cold. Peel off the shells.

Divide the oxtail mixture into 6 equal portions, weighing them for accuracy, if you like. Roll out each one between 2 sheets of cling film so that it is big enough to wrap round an egg. Lightly flour the eggs, then wrap each one in a piece of the oxtail mixture, rolling it up in the cling film as you go and making sure that it is evenly covered, without any gaps. Twist the ends of the cling film tightly to help shape the eggs.

Put the remaining egg in a shallow bowl and beat well. Put the remaining flour in another bowl and the breadcrumbs in a third. Remove the cling film, then dip the Scotch eggs first into the flour, then into the beaten egg and finally into the breadcrumbs, patting them on well with your hands.

Heat the oil to 170°C in a deep-fat fryer or a large, deep saucepan (if you use a saucepan, don't fill it more than a third full, or you risk it boiling over). Add the Scotch eggs to the hot oil, cooking them in batches so as not to overcrowd the pan. Fry for 7–8 minutes, until they are a deep golden brown, then drain well on kitchen paper. Serve warm.

Lobster Omelette Victoria with Lobster Bisque

Lobster, lobster oil, lobster sauce. This is as grand, rich and mighty as the eponymous Queen. Again the flavours are strong, so don't feel you have to use native lobster.

You will need at least 2–3 cooked lobsters for this dish and you can get good lobster oil online.

Serves 4

40g unsalted butter
400g cooked lobster meat, chopped
8 eggs, lightly beaten
salt and freshly ground black pepper

For the béchamel sauce
10g unsalted butter
10g plain flour
50ml milk
20ml double cream
10ml lobster bisque (see page 32)
1 large egg yolk

To garnish (optional)
2 teaspoons lobster oil

First make the sauce. Melt the butter in a small pan and stir in the flour. Gradually add the milk and cream, whisking constantly. Stir in the bisque and simmer for 5 minutes over a low heat. Season well. Take off the heat and leave to cool a little, then whisk in the egg yolk.

Heat the butter in a saucepan, add the lobster and cook gently for 1–2 minutes. Add the eggs, season well and cook over a low heat until softly scrambled.

Transfer the mixture to 4 individual gratin dishes and pour over the béchamel sauce. Place under a hot grill until glazed, then serve immediately, garnished with a drizzle of lobster oil.

Fortnum's Steak Sandwich

A steak sandwich, Fortnum's style. Put under pressure. Literally. The sandwich was traditionally pressed, so that the steak juices and mustard would seep into the bread. You want decent white bread. And minute steak, cooked rare. Fortnum's use Glenarm beef, which is aged in a Himalayan salt chamber. Sounds a little strange but the flavour is astounding. Plus English mustard-spiked butter, for a much-needed kick. And don't forget to press. That's where the magic lies.

Serves 4

- 2 Little Gem lettuces, thinly shredded
- 6 tablespoons good-quality mayonnaise
- 3 tablespoons chopped tarragon
- a little olive oil
- 4 x 120g minute steaks, cut from a sirloin
- 12 slices of square white tin bread
- 8 teaspoons horseradish cream
- 4 plum tomatoes, sliced
- 4 large pickled gherkins, sliced lengthwise
- salt and freshly ground black pepper

For the mustard butter

- 75g softened unsalted butter
- 2 teaspoons English mustard
- a few drops of Worcestershire sauce

Beat together all the ingredients for the mustard butter and set aside. Mix the shredded lettuce with the mayonnaise, tarragon and some salt and black pepper.

Rub a little olive oil on to the steaks and season them well. Sear on a preheated griddle or in a heavy-based frying pan for 1–2 minutes on each side, until they are done to your liking. Remove from the pan and leave to rest in a warm place for 5 minutes while you toast the bread.

To assemble each sandwich, spread 2 slices of toast with the mustard butter. Slice the steak and put it on one of the buttered slices of toast. Top with 2 teaspoons of horseradish cream and then with some of the lettuce. Add the second piece of buttered toast. Layer on top of that some sliced tomato, gherkin and more lettuce. Top with a third piece of toast. Press down firmly for 10 seconds. Then skewer with 4 wooden cocktail sticks near the corners and cut into quarters with a sharp knife.

Oeufs Drumkilbo

Said to be born from a late-night culinary emergency. Guests arrive late at grand Scottish estate, and there's no food. So chef is awoken and creates the dish from what is left in the icebox. Which involves, naturally, lobster and prawns. Those were the days. It was a great favourite of the Queen Mother's, and is suitably rich and regal. Serve in Martini glasses.

Serves 4

- 300g cooked king prawns, roughly diced
- 600g cooked lobster, roughly diced
- 2 plum tomatoes, skinned, deseeded and cut into small dice
- 4 hard-boiled eggs, peeled and diced
- a double quantity of Marie Rose Sauce (see page 84)
- 1 tablespoon olive oil
- 30g pea shoots
- salt and freshly ground black pepper
- brown bread and butter, to serve

Mix the prawns and half the lobster with the diced tomatoes and hard-boiled eggs. Gently fold in the Marie Rose sauce. Divide the mixture between 4 glasses or glass serving dishes.

Put the remaining lobster into a bowl and toss with the olive oil and pea shoots. Season well and put on top of the Marie Rose mixture. Serve with brown bread and butter.

Roasted Marrowbones with Parsley Salt, Parmesan and Shallot Sauce

A dish based on that old classic, devilled bones. The best are hewn from the middle of a calf's leg, and you may have to order them in advance from your butcher. Get them cut into 5cm rounds. For the truly committed, a marrow spoon makes light work of scraping out every last wobbling chunk from the bone. But a teaspoon or knife will do just fine.

Serves 4

100g coarse sea salt
20g flat-leaf parsley leaves
60g salted butter
4 shallots, finely diced
200ml good-quality chicken stock
12 pieces of veal marrowbone, about 5cm thick
4 slices of sourdough bread, toasted
50g Parmesan cheese, grated

Put the salt and parsley into a food processor and whiz until the mixture is a good green colour. Transfer to a bowl and set aside (you can keep any excess parsley salt in a cupboard and use to season all kinds of dishes).

Melt the butter in a shallow pan over a medium heat. Add the shallots and cook gently until they are tender but not coloured. Pour in the chicken stock and simmer for about 5 minutes, until reduced and slightly glossy.

Put the marrowbones on a baking sheet lined with baking parchment and place in an oven heated to 180°C/Gas Mark 4. Cook for 12–20 minutes, depending on the thickness of the bones. You can check by putting a knife through the marrow; it should slide through without any resistance and feel warm to the touch when you remove it.

Once the bones are cooked, divide them between 4 warm serving plates. Serve accompanied by the toasted sourdough, with the parsley salt, Parmesan and shallot sauce in small dishes. The idea is that you dig out a little marrow with a knife or a teaspoon, put it on the toast and add a smidgen of parsley salt, a sprinkling of Parmesan and a little shallot sauce. It's very rich and tastes divine.

Devilled Lamb's Kidneys

Now we're talking, a serious breakfast or supper with a good whack of spice. Devilled simply means a bit of heat, from cayenne pepper, mustard or Worcestershire sauce. Or, in the case of this dish, all three. In Victorian and Edwardian times, very little in the St James's Clubs wasn't devilled . . . bones, eggs, mushrooms and the rest.

The key is to clean and core the kidneys (and lamb's have a wonderfully delicate sweetness when fresh) and cook them so they're still blushing pink within. Overcook, and you get meaty chewing gum. If you feel there's not enough devil, simply ramp up the cayenne pepper.

Serves 4

8 lamb's kidneys
milk, to cover
40g unsalted butter
1 banana shallot, finely chopped
a small bunch of thyme
1 teaspoon cracked black pepper
70ml sherry vinegar
45ml white wine
40g demerara sugar
¼ teaspoon cayenne pepper
a large splash of Worcestershire sauce
120ml good-quality chicken stock
25g grain mustard
150ml double cream
4 large slices of sourdough bread, toasted
salt and freshly ground black pepper

Cut the lamb's kidneys in half and snip out the white core with scissors. Put them into a bowl, pour over enough milk to cover and leave for an hour. Drain well and pat dry.

Melt the butter in a frying pan. When it is foaming, add the kidneys and fry over a medium heat for 2–3 minutes on each side, until well coloured. Remove from the pan and leave to rest.

Add the shallot to the pan and sweat until softened. Stir in the thyme sprigs and cracked black pepper, then add the sherry vinegar, white wine, demerara sugar, cayenne pepper and Worcestershire sauce. Simmer until reduced by half. Pour in the chicken stock and reduce by half again. Stir in the mustard and cream, bring to the boil and simmer until slightly thickened. Season to taste.

Remove the thyme sprigs, if you like, then return the kidneys to the sauce and heat through for 2 minutes. Serve on the sourdough toast.

Cheese Fondue

A 70s' dish that has fallen undeservedly out of fashion. But was hugely popular when served up at The Lodge, a Fortnum & Mason outdoor pop-up which accompanies 'Skate' at Somerset House. Best served in the classic fondue set that usually sits at the back of your cupboard gathering dust. An Alpine classic, and rightly so.

Serves 4

1 garlic clove, peeled
1 teaspoon cornflour
300ml Muscadet sur Lie wine
300g Beaufort cheese, grated
200g Comté cheese, grated
80g Reblochon cheese, grated
50ml kirsch
freshly ground black pepper
cubes of baguette or sourdough bread, to serve

Rub the inside of a fondue pot with the peeled garlic clove – if you don't have a fondue set use a heavy-based saucepan instead.

Mix the cornflour to a paste with a spoonful or two of the wine. Add the remaining wine to the pot or pan and bring to the boil. Stir in the cornflour mixture and reduce the heat to a simmer. Add the grated Beaufort and Comté and let them melt slowly, stirring frequently. Add the grated Reblochon and let that melt in too. Finish by adding the kirsch.

Season with a little black pepper and serve straight away, using fondue forks to dip the bread cubes into the fondue. If you have made it in an ordinary saucepan, you will probably have to return it to the heat now and again to stop it becoming too thick for dipping.

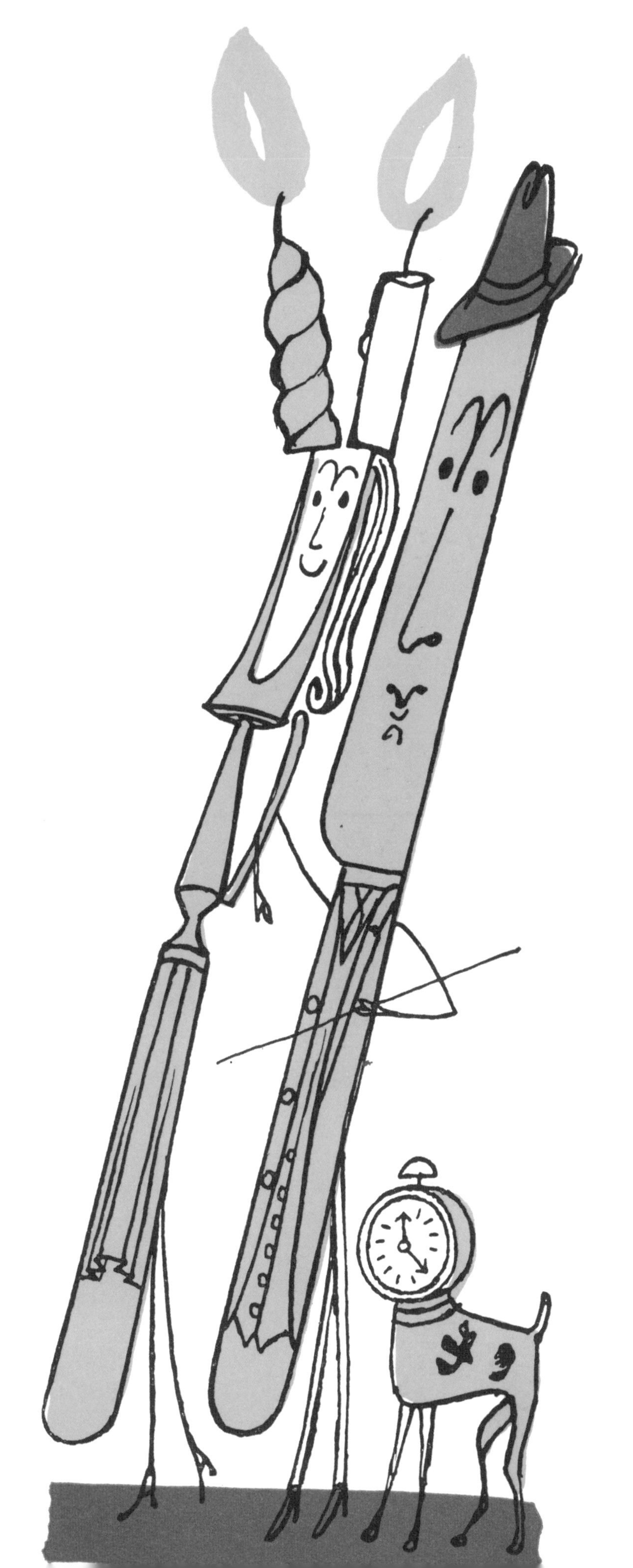

Cocktails

‘We became intoxicated with happiness. We danced. We sang. Several post-Conquest assistants became betrothed. Others remained unbetrothed. All seemed equally delighted’

Martini

The classic cocktail, and traditionally made with gin. And purists will argue (purists always do) that it should ONLY be made with gin. Also, it should be dry, drier than a sauna in the Kalahari. Which means the bare minimum of vermouth. There are endless tales of how to make it suitably arid. Some say that all that is needed is to ring New York, putting the gin bottle at one end of the line, and the vermouth at the other. Others claim that simply letting the sun shine through the vermouth into the cocktail glass is enough. I like to swill the glass (which must be small – there's nothing worse than a warm Martini) with vermouth, and throw away the excess.

And do keep your gin and glasses in the freezer. The great Martini should be freezing cold, viscous and pack a satisfying punch.

Classic Dry Martini

65ml gin or vodka
5ml dry vermouth (Fortnum's use Noilly Prat)
ice cubes
1 olive

Pour the gin or vodka and the vermouth into a chilled mixing glass and add some ice cubes. Stir for 10–15 seconds, then strain into a chilled coupe glass and garnish with an olive (or whatever you prefer).

Martini 45

65ml gin, preferably Hepple gin
5ml dry vermouth (Fortnum's use Noilly Prat)
2.5ml Palo Cortado sherry
ice cubes
a strip of lemon zest
1 olive

Pour the gin, vermouth and sherry into a chilled mixing glass and add some ice cubes. Stir for 10–15 seconds, then strain into a chilled coupe glass. Twist and squeeze a small piece of lemon zest over the drink and garnish with an olive (or the discarded lemon zest).

Negroni

Another cocktail classic, and one that reminds me of soft Italian dusks. Again, with its triple booze hit, this baby is deceptively strong. But the bitterness is sublime, and makes this not only the aperitif of champions, but a pert and pretty palate cleanser too. I always use Campari, but the choice of gin is up to you. As to vermouth, this recipe favours Cocchi Vermouth di Torino. But if you can't find this, then there's nothing wrong with good old Martini Rosso.

25ml Cocchi Vermouth di Torino
25ml gin, preferably East London Liquor dry gin
25ml Campari
ice cubes
a slice of orange

Pour the vermouth, gin and Campari into a chilled mixing glass and add some ice cubes. Stir for 10–15 seconds, then strain into an old-fashioned glass. Add a large ice cube and garnish with the slice of orange.

Sours

The secret to this drink lies in the title. Yup, you've guessed it, you want the lips to pucker, the tongue to recoil, and the brain to freeze for a moment of exquisite surprise. You can use any spirit, but a good Scotch always works wonders for me.

50ml whisky (or spirit of your choice)
25ml lemon juice
15ml sugar syrup
1 egg white
ice cubes
Angostura bitters
a cherry
a strip of lemon zest

Put the first four ingredients into the small half of a mixing tin. Seal the tin and shake for 10–15 seconds, allowing the contents to emulsify. Add some ice cubes and shake hard for 10–15 seconds. Strain into a chilled glass. Add a dash of Angostura bitters over the top to finish. Garnish with the cherry and a strip of lemon zest.

Old Fashioned

Don't muck with perfection. This makes up the third of the great cocktail trio, alongside the Martini and the Negroni. It carries a smooth, elegant punch, and is best sipped in late-night, ill-lit bars.

50ml bourbon
5ml sugar syrup
3 dashes of Angostura bitters
ice cubes
a strip of orange zest
a cherry

Pour the whisky, sugar syrup and Angostura bitters into a chilled mixing glass and add some ice cubes. Stir for 10–15 seconds, then strain into an old-fashioned glass. Add ice cubes and garnish with the strip of orange zest and the cherry.

Classic Champagne Cocktail

This is old-school and blissfully pure. I wouldn't use the really good vintage stuff, rather something a little more mainstream. The Fortnum & Mason house Champagne is excellent value, and far superior to those megastar brands that often promise more than they can deliver.

---

1 white sugar cube
Angostura bitters
25ml Cognac
125ml Champagne
a strip of orange zest

Soak the sugar cube in Angostura bitters and put it into a chilled Champagne glass. Pour in the Cognac and top up with the Champagne. Garnish with the strip of orange zest.

Acknowledgements

Very few cook books are the work of one person. And in the case of a tome like this, it would have been simply impossible to write without the time, advice, wisdom, wit and support of the group of people listed here.

Working with Fortnum & Mason (and 4th Estate) was a joy, not only in terms of sheer slick professionalism, but also experiencing the passion and dedication everyone feels for this wonderful shop and brand.

The whole process was a rare delight. And god, I learnt a lot. Although meetings where tea is served in a bag, rather than individual pot, and mug, rather than bone china cup, might take some getting used to. Hey ho. Such is the Fortnum's way. Without the people below, there would be no book. I had the easy part of collating many centuries of expertise. The real hard work was done by you. So a heartfelt and Fortnum & Mason-sized thank you.

Kate Hobhouse, The Weston family, Ewan Venters, Zia Zareem-Slade, Sydney Aldridge, Dr Andrea Tanner, Polly Long, Yvonne Isherwood, Natalia Matusik, Julien Lanclume, Joan Duncan, Jason Kavanagh, Scott Stewart Villacora, Lee Streeton, James Randall, Jonathan Hamilton, Sam Rosen Nash, Clare Henshaw, Ellie Price, David Loftus, Francesca Anderson, Jo Harris, Jess Lea-Wilson, Jane Middleton, Florence Holzapfel, Ed Victor, Sam Wolfson, Gary Simpson, Julian Humphries, Louise Haines, Sarah Thickett, Louise Tucker, Michelle Kane, Matt Clacher.

Credits

Illustrations

The illustrations in this book come from the Fortnum & Mason archive. The Edward Bawden pictures are reproduced with the kind permission of the Estate and Peyton Skipwith.

p. iv: by appointment, Edward Bawden, *Christmas Catalogue* (1958).

p. 3: woman with fruit hat, Edward Bawden, *Another Invitation to Indulgence* (1958).

p. 6: cat with ingredients, Edward Bawden, *Christmas Catalogue* (1958).

pp. 8-9: couple eating breakfast, Edward Bawden, *Christmas Catalogue* (1956).

p. 15: chicken and eggs, Edward Bawden, *Easter Leaflet* (1956).

p. 23: fish and duck, Edward Bawden, *Invitation to Indulgence* (1958).

pp. 28-9: lobster in top hat, W. M. Hendy, *Entertaining Made Easy* (April 1938).

p. 37: The Presentable Cat, Edward Bawden, *Christmas Catalogue* (1958).

pp. 38-9: cat and dog fighting over sausage, Edward Bawden, *Christmas Catalogue* (1958).

pp. 46-7: elephant, Edward Bawden, *Christmas Catalogue* (1955).

p. 49: The Most Famous Tea Counter in the World, W. M. Hendy, *flyer* (c. 1932).

pp. 56-7: ants with biscuits, Edward Bawden, *Invitation to Indulgence* (1957).

p. 61: bees, Edward Bawden, *Invitation to Indulgence* (1958).

p. 65: woman with cat and teapots, Edward Bawden, *Another Invitation to Indulgence* (1958).

pp. 68-9: pianist and musicians, Edward Bawden, *Entertaining à la Carte* (c. 1959).

p. 71: fish on plate with sea/fisherman, Edward Bawden, *Entertaining à la Carte* (c. 1959).

p. 91: tree full of peacocks and people, Edward Bawden, *The Delectable History of Fortnum & Mason* (1957).

p. 93: fish with top hat, Stuart Menzies, *Store Cupboard Spring list. Hoorah! It's Coronation Year* (1937).

p. 99: couple with picnic, Edward Bawden, *Good Things to Eat and Other Delicacies for Summer Days* (June 1957).

p. 109: man pulling turnip, Edward Bawden, *Invitation to Indulgence* (1958).

pp. 110-11: Neptune and mermaid, (artist unknown), *Ices catalogue* (May 1937).

p. 112: mermaid, W. M. Hendy, *Condiments from Far Cathay catalogue* (April 1931).

pp. 126-27: teapot and coffee pot couple, Edward Bawden, *Invitation to Indulgence* (1958).

p. 145: woman icing a cake plus cat, Edward Bawden, *Christmas Catalogue* (1956).

p. 157: couple with winged waiters, R. Taylor, *Entertaining Made Easy* (c. 1935).

p. 158: cat with caviar tin, Edward Bawden, *Christmas Catalogue* (1958).

p. 167: feeding the fish on a lazy Susan, Edward Bawden, *Everything for Cocktails and Cocktail Parties* (February 1936).

p. 169: birds drinking with decanter, Edward Bawden, *Invitation to Indulgence* (1958).

p. 173: dining room and footmen, Edward Bawden, *Everything for Cocktails and Cocktail Parties* (February 1936).

p. 177: cow drinking beef tea, Edward Bawden, *Feeling Fit; Invalid Delicacies* (c. 1935).

p. 185: lobster and crab with candles, Edward Bawden, *Christmas Catalogue* (1957).

p. 198: couple in booth with wine, Edward Bawden, *Fortnum & Mason Pierce the Gloom* (1958).

pp. 204-05: couple at table, with musicians, W. M. Hendy, *Jubilee Commentary* (1935).

p. 211: man with watering can, Edward Bawden, *Winsome Ideas* (1932).

p. 218: cauliflower with worm, Edward Bawden, *Another Invitation to Indulgence* (1958).

p. 221: list of monarchs and harp, Edward Bawden, *Christmas Catalogue* (1958).

pp. 226-27: cat with bird hat, Edward Bawden, *Christmas Catalogue* (1958).

p. 230: marching fruit, (artist unknown, though possibly W. M. Hendy), *Come Let Us Command Fortnum & Mason to Put Auntie on Her Feet Again* (c. 1932).

p. 234: crowned strawberry woman, W. M. Hendy, *Everything for Your Store Cupboard* (October 1930).

p. 240: children playing in tree, Edward Bawden, *Invitation to Indulgence* (1958).

pp. 250-51: Dr Johnson and Mrs Thrale, W. M. Hendy, *Christmas Catalogue* (1932).

p. 253: Christmas stocking, Edward Bawden, *Christmas Catalogue* (1956).

p. 255: levitating waiter, W. M. Hendy, *Commentary on Dainties to Fit You for the Stress of Autumn* (1930).

p. 257: couple with fish heads, Edward Bawden, *Fortnum & Mason Pierce the Gloom* (1958).

p. 258: Fortnum & Mason Humpty Dumpty, Edward Bawden, *Easter Flyer* (1958).

p. 263: Fortnum's Easter egg, Edward Bawden, *Easter Flyer* (1957).

p. 275: cutlery, candles, clock, Edward Bawden, *Christmas Catalogue* (1957).

pp. 276-77: cat couple drinking, Edward Bawden, *Christmas Catalogue* (1958).

p. 291: Triumph, R. Taylor, *Hurrah! Summer is a Comin-In! Fortnum & Mason's Store Cupboard Commentary, Spring* (March 1938).

Quotation credits

Chapter opener quotes on p. 2, p. 46, p. 110, p. 126, p. 156, p. 172, p. 210, p. 226, p. 254 and p. 276 all from catalogues in the Fortnum & Mason archive. Chapter opener quote on p. 68 from John le Carré, *The Mission Song*, Hodder & Stoughton, 1996.

Other credits

Much of the photography in this book was shot on location at 181 Piccadilly behind a shop hoarding on the third floor.

Index